Mother Maiden Crone

SHAMANIC CEREMONIES FOR WOMEN'S
TRANSITIONS: A FACILITATOR'S GUIDEBOOK

Nancy D. Baker, PhD, DMs

Copyright © 2013 Nancy D. Baker, PhD, DMs
All rights reserved.

ISBN-10: 1482022370
EAN-13: 9781482022377

Library of Congress Control Number: 2013901205
CreateSpace Independent Publishing Platform
North Charleston, South Carolina

Table of Contents

Acknowledgements	v
Introduction	vii
Chapter 1: Winding Our Way Through Some Literature	1
General Literature	2
Transitions with a Focus on Women	4
Specific Aspects of Shamanic Ceremonies	7
Summary of Literature	9
Chapter 2: The Ceremony Template	13
Basic Shamanic Ceremony Template	13
The General Flow of the Ceremony Experience	15
Preparation Meeting and Preparation Period	15
Arrival on the Day of the Ceremony and Ceremony Set-Up	16
The Beginning of the Ceremony	19
The Ceremony Proper	21
The End of the Ceremony	21
A Note on the Use of Spiritual Tools	22
Chapter 3: The Shamanic Ceremonies	25
The Birth of a Girl Child	29
Preparation Meeting and Preparation Period	29
The Beginning of the Ceremony	29
The Ceremony Proper	33
The End of the Ceremony	41

The Honoring of Self and Fertility 45
Preparation Meeting and Preparation Period 45
The Beginning of the Ceremony 46
The Ceremony Proper 50
The End of the Ceremony 59

The Becoming of an Adult Woman 63
Preparation Meeting and Preparation Period 63
The Beginning of the Ceremony 64
The Ceremony Proper 68
The End of the Ceremony 78

Negotiating the Mid-Life Transition 81
Preparation Meeting and Preparation Period 81
The Beginning of the Ceremony 82
The Ceremony Proper 86
The End of the Ceremony 95

Menopause, the Birth of the Crone 99
Preparation Meeting and Preparation Period 99
The Beginning of the Ceremony 100
The Ceremony Proper 104
The End of the Ceremony 115

The Death of the Crone 119
Preparation Meeting and Preparation Period 119
The Beginning of the Ceremony 120
The Ceremony Proper 124
The End of the Ceremony 130

Chapter 4: Thoughts and Musings 133

Bibliography 139

About the Author 143

About the Photographer 145

Acknowledgements

I wish to acknowledge all of the individuals who have taught me how to connect deeply within, on this Earthly realm, whether they are aware of their teaching or not. Even more, however, I would like to acknowledge my Inner Guides, both Inner Beings and Animals. They knew the way; they have the map. They taught me where to go, and how to go, so that I might be an Inner Journeyer.

Further, I am thankful for my farm, Piper Hill Farm, in Pennsylvania. Without all the hard manual work, and all of the time outside no matter what the weather, I would not have 'found' the Earth, and all that is contained within it, nor the Universe, and all that there is to be.

I look forward to opening more doors, to Other Realms, with continued guidance from teachers of eternal wisdom.

Introduction

Mother, Maiden, Crone...The birth of a daughter. A celebration. A young girl, a daughter, marking her first menstrual period, standing between the women who love and support her. Celebrating. Or a girl, becoming an adult, between the women who lovingly guide her. Women supporting and guiding the next generation. Or those women, as their roles in life change from young adult roles to their next ones, no longer focused on young adult societal demands, transitioning into what has been called the midlife crisis. Or the woman entering menopause, another major transition, this time to Wise Woman, the Crone. What an accomplishment! One that is neither supported nor recognized, but rather is often full of physical and emotional angst. This time, instead, surrounded by women who are walking the same, but different, paths. Young and old celebrating that transition with her. Then, the woman walking and passing from the sunset of her life to the winter; the death. Not alone, but with other women, as her Spirit reunites with the One. With other women celebrating what she has given and not forgetting her memory; celebrating her. Celebrating, and holding On High, the person, the woman, the Soul. And the cycle of life continues for the next woman, and the next; the never ending cycle of the female that repeats itself every time a girl child is born.

Certainly it is not easy for both men and women to connect to either their deep core Self or the sacred

Divine within themselves. In addition, as the individual transitions from being a child, into an adolescent, into an adult, into middle age, and then into his or her older age, there are no longer societal markers that support and hold sacred those transitional milestones. There are no ceremonial rituals in our modern cultures. Often individuals bumble through them, resulting in negative rather than positive transitions. Additionally, in a male-dominated society such as ours, it is even more difficult for a woman to be successful at these tasks and transitions.

This guidebook will present literature related to ceremony and detail a basic general template for conducting a Shamanic Ceremony. Then, using that template, it will detail complete ceremonies that mark the major transitions in the life of a woman, beginning with the birth of the girl child and ending with the death of the Crone. These ceremonies can be powerful markers for a woman's life transitions and can be used, as cultures in the past had regularly done, to support and to facilitate these transitions. From these ceremonies it will be clear that women can celebrate both their female-ness and their transitions.

This guidebook will afford an individual facilitator all she needs to conduct the ceremonies detailed within this book. From the first call asking for a ceremony, through an initial meeting, and then the complete ceremony, you will feel confident in conducting the ceremonies as is or modifying them to meet your needs or personality.

Chapter 1

Winding Our Way Through Some Literature

This summary of literature is done in four sections. The first presents literature that covers general ritual and ceremony to provide a basic foundation of understanding. The second section focuses on literature that covers women undergoing life transitions. The third section summarizes literature that covers specific aspects of ceremony directly related to these Shamanic Ceremonies. The final section summarizes the literature.

General Literature

The following books were helpful in designing the ceremonies presented in this guidebook. They are beneficial for the guide wishing to explore further the topic of ceremony. *The Joy Of Ritual* (Biziou, 1999) is written in a simple format that describes how to create and present various types of rituals. These include: everyday rituals such as Inner Guidance and Purification; Rites of Passage rituals such as New Year, New Home, and Retirement; moving through stressful times such as Moving Through Depression and Releasing Negativity; rituals for relationships such as Bringing in Love and Revitalizing Love; rituals of connection such as Appreciating Coworkers and Honoring Ancestors; rituals for health such as Healing the Self and Dealing with Grief; women's rituals such as Finding Your Power and Grieving the Unborn; and men's rituals such as Connecting with Father and Appreciating the Feminine.

Especially helpful are the sections in which the author clearly lays out directions on how to create a ceremony, from the elements of a ritual to 'tools of the trade.' This 'tools of the trade' chapter gives nice thumbnail sketches of utensils such as candles, aromas, food and drink, crystals and gemstones, and the elements, with totem information for all. It is a good overall, clearly-written survey book that also offers reference for those called to conduct ceremonies.

A more in-depth book on creating ceremonies is *Sacred Ceremony: How to Create Ceremonies for Healing, Transitions, and Celebrations* (Farmer, 2002). The author reviews the process of sacred ceremony and tools, and then presents ceremonies for healing such as Release and Renewal Healing and Community Healing, transition such as Marriage Ceremonies and Farewells, and celebration such as Earth Seasons and Celestial Cycles and Solar Cycles and Seasons.

The Book of Ceremonies: A Native Way of Honoring and Living the Sacred, Gabriel Horn (Horn, 2000) presents similar information as the book listed above but from a native perspective with a significant amount of native folklore and writings. Ceremonies are presented from an Earth-based, circular perspective versus linear, symbolic one. The author presents ceremonies for marriage, death, and the seasons, but also includes ceremonies for dreams and visions, such as Crying for the Vision and Ceremony for the Dream.

Neo Pagan Rites: A Guide to Creating Public Rituals that Work (Bonewits, 2007) presents information from the Neo Pagan perspective. There is a chapter in which terms are defined so all are aware of what the author defines as Neo Pagan and worship, accordingly. The rest of the book offers a significant amount of information on how to write and conduct a ceremony in the Neo Pagan manner. Henry Close (Close, 2006) writes about ceremony from the Christian perspective in *Ceremonies for Spiritual Healing and Growth*. Close details ceremonies that he conducts, categorized as ceremonies for healing, such as Support for a Rape Survivor and Forgiving Another Person, and life cycles, such as Marriage and Grieving.

Finally, Susan Mumm (Mumm, 2004), in her book, *The Rituals Resource Book: Alternative Weddings, Funerals, Holidays and Other Rites of Passage*, presents her ceremonies with a feeling of anti-establishment. This perspective is fairly pervasive throughout and can take away from the message if one gets caught up in her negative feelings about tradition and traditional ceremonies. However, there are a significant number of ceremonies that she presents including Alternative Marriage, Funeral and Holiday Rituals, as well as Parenting Partnership Ceremony and Adulthood Rites of Passage ceremonies.

Transitions with a Focus on Women

The following literatures on two specific population groups, adolescents and adult females progressing through life transitions, were used for development of the ceremonies presented in this guidebook. They are helpful in understanding the individuals for whom the ceremonies are written.

Crossroads: The Quest for Contemporary Rites of Passage (Mahdi, Christopher, & Meade, 1996) presents many authors' writings on adolescence and rites of passage and how our culture is negatively affected by its lack of culturally-sanctioned rites of passages. The various authors make the point that if not presented with cultural rites of passage, adolescents will create their own, often leading to negative transitions, such as participation in gangs and violence. The editors then present

Winding Our Way Through Some Literature

current local-specific rites of passage, both for groups and individuals.

The Thundering Years: Rituals and Sacred Wisdom for Teens (Johnson, 2001), is written for teens as well as adults. It helps guide the teen through the 'thundering years,' by incorporating practices and exercises, all presented in a flowing, caring manner. It is an excellent book for a high school class or any group to use as a basis for creating and conducting either a group or individual Rites of Passage.

Two books dealing with mentoring girls into womanhood are worth mentioning. The first, *Daughters of the Moon, Sisters of the Sun: Young Women & Mentors on the Transition to Womanhood* (Hughes & Wolf, 1997) is a wonderful volume that integrates essays written by girls with adult women mentors. For example, in "The Emerging Self," 13-year old Heather Wolf-Smeeth writes about her growing and developing sense of Self. This is followed with a discussion written by Carol Gilligan, a well-known Harvard University professor and author. This section continues with a total of nine essays, alternating between the adolescents' essays and the mentors' essays. The topic areas covered in this book are The Emerging Self, Taking it to the Edge, Growing Up Fast and Speaking Out, Finding Our Power, and Gendertalks. This is a good book for mother-daughter dyads to read together and any individual or group focusing on adolescent females developing into young women.

In the book, *Becoming Peers: Mentoring Girls into Womanhood*, the author (L'am, 2006) specifically deals with reflections and ceremony related to a girl's first menstruation, as well as with women's continuing menstruation. L'am describes how, as an adult, she began using cloth menstrual pads, and how this act connected herself to her body, her blood, the collective blood of menstruating women, the sacredness of that blood, and of viewing it as a 'substance that nourishes life,' rather than something negative (p. 14). It is an incredible journey of connecting to the sacred female. She goes on to describe creating ceremonies in general, and then creating ceremonies specifically related to adolescents beginning menstruation and those mentoring these girls.

Further reading on the topic of celebrating menstruation includes the book *105 Ways to Celebrate Menstruation* (McBride, 2004). In this book McBride attempts to change how women perceive menstruation and, thus, internalize the physiological body process in a new, more positive way. The author tries to teach women to celebrate menstruation.

Finally, *The Seven Sacred Rites of Menopause: The Spiritual Journey to the Wise-Woman Years* (Boylan, 2000), delves into the end of menstruation, or menopause. Boylan begins by detailing her own misunderstood journey through menopause, a phenomena that is, sadly, not unusual. From her experience, Boylan wrote this spiritual guide so that other women might negotiate this process in a more sacred manner by becoming and celebrating the Crone.

Specific Aspects of Shamanic Ceremonies

Water as Healing. Three books on the importance, the symbolism, and the use of water in ceremony are mentioned here for the guide to understand why water energy work is included within the context of the ceremonies presented in the coming chapters.

Spiritual Bathing: Healing Rituals and Traditions from Around the World (Arvigo & Epstein, 2003) is a beautiful book that presents the spiritual uses of water from different cultures and describes water rituals that the reader can employ. The authors review cultural groups such as the Jews, the Sumerians and Egyptians, Christians, Ancient Romans and Greeks, Muslims, Celts, Finns, Russians, and Native Americans. For example, in the chapter presenting the Hindus 'Rivers of the Goddess,' the spiritual aspect of water and how the Hindi use the Ganges is presented, followed by an explanation of swimming and bathing rituals one can use on his or her own.

There is some overlap of historical information in *Sacred Water: The Spiritual Source of Life* (Altman, 2002); however, the layout of the book is much different. Altman includes no presentations of how to use water in ceremony oneself, but the sacredness of water is reviewed within categories such as cleansing, healing, initiation, wisdom, and enchantment. This book contains much more historical information within these topics, and taken together, the two books give a good background on the historical and cultural uses of water in a spiritual sense.

A third book dealing with water, *The Sweat Lodge is for Everyone* (McGarvie, 2009) specifically addresses the cleansing aspect of water, in terms of a sweat lodge. As part of her review, the author presents historic evidence of the use of sweat lodges from different cultures around the world, and then more specifically, the Native American use. She details the building of a sweat lodge and performing sweat lodge ceremonies.

Shamanism. The foundational element, the main underlying component of the ceremonies presented in this guidebook, is Shamanism. How Shamanism is incorporated into these ceremonies specifically, is detailed in the following chapter, in the section called, Basic Shamanic Ceremony Template.

However, for those feeling that they need more information specific to Shamanism, the following books provide a solid foundation in understanding what Shamanism is, as well as how Shamans journey within the Inner Realms: *Shamanic Journeying: A Beginner's Guide* (Ingerman, 2004), *Shamanic Healing within the Medicine Wheel* (Lorler, 1998), *Walkers between the Worlds: The Western Mysteries from Shaman to Magus* (Matthews & Matthews, 2003), *The Complete Idiot's Guide to Celtic Wisdom* (McColman, 2003), and *The Invisible Landscape: Mind, Hallucinogen, and the iChing* (McKenna & McKenna, 1993).

If the guide is interested in a complete review of all aspects of Shamanism, there is an outstanding book by Roger Walsh, *The World of Shamanism: New Views of an*

Ancient Tradition (Walsh, 2010). This book is comprehensive and full of information, both from past and current understandings of Shamanism.

Summary of Literature

Overall, the above literature is in agreement on what ceremonies and rituals are. People partake in rituals on many occasions, often in an unconscious manner, from their bedtime routine to the repetitive spiritual routines in church services.

What this guidebook focuses on are the conscious rituals or ceremonies. Conscious ceremonies can be powerful. It is thought that within ceremony one joins the metaphysical with the physical. It is a means of calling the Divine into our lives (Biziou, 1999). Various concepts are used to describe the process of ceremony: shifting consciousness and entering a state of grace (Biziou, 1999); renewal and inspiration and joyous celebration (Mumm, 2004); non-ordinary states of consciousness from which the individual is able to move beyond his or her typical limitations (Grof, 1998); giving form to intention; and giving the internal state an external expression (L'am, 2006). L'am explains that part of the power of ceremony is that we create an internal event that is experienced by our spirit, or Self, as a 'lived reality' which then begins to be defined by our intention (p. 28).

But even more than general ceremonies, this guidebook details those that specifically address Rites of Passage. This type of ceremony can be the bridge over which one walks when transitioning from one life phase to another (Farmer, 2002).

In his chapter, Guidelines For Creating Effective Rites Of Passage, Robert Eckert (Eckert, 1998) describes in-depth the elements of an effective Rite of Passage ceremony. He states that there must be strong standards for a Rite of Passage for a youth, elders must be present, and there needs to be congruence between all participants. Then, there must be a non-ordinary state of consciousness reached, what he believes holds the power of the ritual, a connection to something greater than the individual. He further believes there must be some sort of death to the old and rebirth to the new experience, so that the individual is able to step into the new role and make the 'passage.' The guide needs to be healthy emotionally and spiritually, as well as clear about what the purpose of the ceremony is, while the participant must have a sincere desire to share in the rite. Eckert states that there must be a period of preparation, and it would be helpful to have an outward symbol of the completion of the passage.

L'am (L'am, 2006) presents her viewpoint of the stages of ceremony very simply. She discusses three stages. First is the invocation, the beginning, where the sacred space is opened and ordinary reality ends. This can be as simple as an announcement that the ceremony is beginning. Second is the body of the ceremony, where the internal state and intention become reality. This is the ceremony proper. Third, is the closing, which is just as important as the opening of the ceremony. L'am states that not only does it close the sacred, but it also helps the participants transition back into reality.

Put into other words, there needs to be a clear intention, a purpose. Once the ceremony is ready to begin, there is an overt, and maybe even symbolic, beginning, such as a candle being lit. This symbol signals to the participants that it is time to leave ordinary life behind and step into the sacred. The middle is the ceremony proper, where the work is done. This is the time when there is release and renewal, death and rebirth, or initiation (Farmer, 2002). The ceremony ends, as it began, with a marker that symbolizes the closing.

Chapter 2

The Ceremony Template

Basic Shamanic Ceremony Template

As part of this guidebook, a basic Shamanic ceremony template is described in this chapter. Six Shamanic ceremonies for women's life transitions, based on this template, are detailed in the next chapter.

The template includes a preliminary meeting which occurs prior to the ceremony itself, during which the intention and purpose are clearly discussed and defined.

For the actual ceremony, the marker that it is beginning is an invocation during which candles are lit. Among other tasks, the ceremony proper will contain a Shamanic Journey, a time of reflection and discussion. The end of the ceremony will be marked by the extinguishing of the candles, along with a statement that the ceremony is over. As an outward symbol of the ceremony experience, all participants will take home a washcloth used in the spiritual cleansing which they decorated during the reflective, processing period.

What sets these ceremonies apart from typical ceremonies is the Shamanic aspect. This aspect occurs in three places: first, in the choice of and manner that candles are included in both the beginning and end of the ceremonies; second, their lighting being embedded within a short Shamanic Journey; and third, within the body of each ceremony there is a full Shamanic Journey.

Shamans are individuals who are able to connect and travel in the Inner Realms, generally through the use of trance states or ritual. These individuals connect the human plane with the spiritual. As part of the connecting, they routinely 'work' with Inner Guides, animal totems, spirits or Beings, and the elemental energies of Earth, Air, Fire, and Water. The practice of Shamanism is one of the earliest spiritual traditions, and as such, is very connected to nature, the elements, and to the cycles of life, nature, the sun, and the moon.

Within these ceremonies, the first journey facilitates the opening of the elemental energy flow, bringing it to the outer realms, using candles to mark that opening. Of all of the elemental energies opened, Water energy will be utilized the most during all of the ceremonies. Moon energy will be used as well. Both of these have female aspects and are seen as important for a woman's life transitions. Additionally, in each ceremony, the guide will take the participants on a Shamanic Journey specific to the woman's life transition that is being celebrated. A final journey will close the flow of the elemental energies. Extinguishing the candles will mark the closing and end of the ceremony.

Thus, the template, and resulting ceremonies, will include a clearly defined beginning, middle, and end. These will all be laid upon a foundation of Shamanism. The topic of the ceremonies will be transitions across the lifespan of the woman.

The General Flow of the Ceremony Experience

This section details for the facilitator, the overall plan for the Shamanic Ceremonies. Any of these instructions can be modified to meet the specific facilitator's needs. The specific instructions for each ceremony are detailed below.

Preparation Meeting and Preparation Period

All important ceremonies have a preparation period of some sort and life transition ceremonies are no different. The preparation helps set the day apart as being different, special, and sacred.

To prepare for the ceremony, engage in a discussion with the participants at least two weeks beforehand. In general, the discussion should include relevant background information, expectations, pre-ceremony preparation, necessary items to bring along, and a general explanation of what will occur during the ceremony.

Essential oils or incense, if used, will be tested or discussed for any scent sensitivities.

An assignment related to the specific life transition will be given during the meeting, as well as pre-ceremony reflection and journaling work. The ceremony should not be scheduled until the individual has completed the assignment. Whether the recommended assignments are utilized is up to the discretion of the facilitator, but at the least, some period of reflection is suggested.

Although there are varying degrees of dietary preparation recommended by different individuals who conduct these types of ceremonies, at the minimum, two days prior to the ceremony, one should eat well with little or no sugar intake and a limit placed on soda and caffeine. Individuals should rest well the night before the ceremony and eat a good breakfast the morning of the ceremony.

Arrival on the Day of the Ceremony and Ceremony Set-Up

There is a meet and greet segment when the participant and any guests arrive. Comfort is addressed, questions answered, and the overall plan of day discussed. Essential oils or incense, to support and enhance inner journeying, if used, are chosen together with the participant and guests.

The following essential oils or incense scents are suggested for use in the ceremonies, either alone or in combination. These can be burned or diffused. Methods of diffusion include putting boiling water into a bowl and adding 1 to 9 drops of the essential oil(s) or using a humidifier, also with 1 to 9 drops. There are also diffusers that one can purchase for use with essential oils. For these and other options, please see Worwood (1991).

These scents were chosen for their qualities that would support and enhance Shamanic inner journeying. Any use, of course, is dependent on any scent sensitivities that any individuals might have, or the preference of the facilitator. The information utilized for essential oil use were contained within these books: *Aromatherapy: A Complete Guide to the Healing Art* (Keville & Green, 2009), *The Complete Book of Essential Oils & Aromatherapy* (Worwood, 1991), and *Essential Aromatherapy: A Pocket Guide to Essential Oils & Aromatherapy* (Worwood & Worwood, 2003), *The Encyclopedia of Psychoactive Plants: Ethnopharmacology and its Applications* (Ratsch, 2005), the essential oil pages from a Shaman website (IAmShaman. com, 2011), and the tools section of *The Joy Of Ritual* (Biziou, 1999).

A list of suggested essential oils and incenses, and a brief summary of why they were chosen for use in the ceremonies, follows.

- Frankincense has a long spiritual history. *The Encyclopedia of Psychoactive Plants: Ethnopharmacology and its Applications* (Ratsch, 2005) details how it was the most important spiritual incense of the ancients, used by Assyrians, Hebrews, Arabs, Egyptians, and Greeks. It also has been and is used by the Catholic Church.

According to Ratsch, it has inebriating, euphoriant, and mood-improving effects.

A summary of its strengths appears on IAMShaman.com (IAmShaman.com, 2011). It is described as calming, centering, and helpful in ceasing mental chatter, worry, and agitation. It opens our spirits to flow, allowing us to let go of our daily life and our hold on the past. It is very useful as a meditation tool.

Additionally, it unites body and spirit and helps one connect with the Divine (Keville & Green, 2009). It also releases anxieties and is useful for spiritual endeavors and meditation (Biziou, 1999).

- Myrrh, often combined with Frankincense, also has spiritual qualities attributed to it. Its strengths include centering, meditative, and visualizing qualities (IAmShaman.com, 2011). It is also described as inspiring of prayer, meditation, and revitalizing of spirit (Keville & Green, 2009).

- Lavender is one of the most widely known and used scents. It is calming and reportedly good for the cleansing of emotional conflicts (Biziou, 1999). With its sedating qualities (Worwood, 1991), it is relaxing and uplifting and balances both mind and body (IAmShaman.com, 2011). Keville & Green (2009) review current research on lavender, stating that the scent affects the adrenal glands as well as the autonomic nervous system, thus illustrating a physiological effect. They also note that lavender balances the emotions and reduces anxiety and distress.

- Rosewood, a less well-known essential oil, has a steadying and balancing effect on emotions (IAmShaman.com, 2011), It also increases tranquility and supports emotional work (Keville & Green, 2009).

- Vetivert Root is also less-known but has relaxing, uplifting, and releasing qualities. It imparts a feeling of security and helps ground and center (Keville & Green, 2009) as well as soothe the mind and body into deep relaxation (IAmShaman.com, 2011).

The Beginning of the Ceremony

Once the scents are chosen and everyone is comfortable, movement into the ceremony proper begins. This beginning phase consists of diffusing the essential oils or lighting the incense, lighting the candles, and opening the sacred space.

You, as guide, will explain that for Shamans the elements of Earth, Air, Fire, and Water are associated with the compass directions. The pairing of element with direction varies by Shamanic tradition. For this ceremony the pairings of direction with element are North-Earth, East-Air, South-Fire, and West-Water, which is common to the Celtic Shaman tradition. Six colored candles are brought forward: brown or green, yellow, red, blue, white, and purple. A compass is placed in a central spot so that all may be aware of the compass directions. Either you or the participants set the candles in their correct locations, with the brown or green one being placed in the North location, the yellow one in the East, red in the South, blue in the West, and white and purple placed in the center. All sit.

You explain that there will be Shamanic InWorld journeys and the participants will be asked to relax, close their eyes, and visualize the words that you say. Express also, that not all people visualize, but rather some sense, some feel, and some just listen; making sure that the participants know that there is no right and wrong to their experiences. Because of the importance of this discussion, this text will also be included in the ceremonies below.

White washcloths are handed out and the participants told that they will use them later. They are directed to put the washcloths on their laps.

You then ask all of the participants to get comfortable and breathe in a relaxed manner. You will begin reading the Shamanic Ceremony opening. As you read the text, presented in the following chapters, read slowly, pausing frequently, allowing the participants the time they need to enter and feel and sense the Inner Realms.

After the completion of the Shamanic Journey to open the ceremony, the Ceremony Proper will begin.

The Ceremony Proper

The text of the actual Shamanic Journey within each of the ceremonies begins with an InWorld spiritual cleansing. The participants are then taken to the West, the realm of Water energy and then to the Upper World of the West, the realm of the Moon. From there, the Shamanic journey focuses on the specific life transition at hand.

In addition to the Shamanic Journey, there may be other tasks for the participants to complete. However, there is always time set aside for processing. It is during this time that the participants are provided dye or other relevant art materials to decorate their white washcloths, which were used in the spiritual cleansing, so that they are able to take home an outward symbol of the ceremony.

The End of the Ceremony

After the Shamanic Journey has concluded, any experiential work is finished, and the ceremony processing completed, the end of the ceremony will take place. This involves extinguishing the essential oil diffusion or incense, closing all of the energy flows that were opened, and extinguishing the candles. To close the energy flow, the participants will be asked once again to sit in a relaxed manner, and you will read the Shamanic Journey that closes the ceremony.

A Note on the Use of Spiritual Tools

Within the Shamanic Ceremonies, I have incorporated the use of some specific spiritual tools. I have found them to be helpful in bringing the spiritual and mystical elements of InWorld Shamanic work to the Outer Realms, to our realms. It is as if the spiritual tool links the two realms, allowing one to hold onto what they have connected to when they were InWorld, so that he or she can reconnect to it at a future time.

One tool that is used in all of the ceremonies is the washcloth, which is used in the InWorld spiritual cleansing part of the ceremony. Later, at the end of the ceremony, during the processing phase, the participants are invited to decorate and take home the washcloth, thereby becoming a personalized reminder of the experience of the ceremony. This allows the participant to use the washcloth at a later time as a memory bridge in order to connect the Outer Realms to their previous Inner Realm Shamanic ceremony experience.

Another tool that is used in some of the Shamanic Ceremonies is a Chartres Labyrinth. Labyrinths are walking meditation tools and are easily incorporated into any kind of ceremony. In a labyrinth, there is one path in, ending up in the center, with the same path as the way out. This distinguishes labyrinths from mazes in which there are multiple paths with an underlying goal of a game. Quite the opposite is the labyrinth, with an underlying goal of peace, relaxed flow, and a calm, meditative state.

Although the process is different from using a washcloth as a tool, walking the labyrinth as part of the ceremony also helps connect the Inner spiritual realms to the Outer Realms, allowing for a greater potential of bringing the experience to the participant's everyday life. In addition they can be very powerful and very healing. Walking a labyrinth slows everything down. Walking with a mantra facilitates the internalization of that mantra to one's being. And when used in conjunction with the sacredness of the ceremony, it heightens the experience.

I would strongly recommend if you do not have one, nor want to make a permanent one, find a way to make a temporary one. For example, you can draw or paint a labyrinth on multiple bed sheets, pin them or sew them into one piece and use it in the ceremonies. Permanent labyrinths can be made of stones, pavers, sand mounds, or any material that does not decompose. Another option is to purchase a portable one online. A common favorite is the Chartres Labyrinth, which is in the floor of a cathedral built in 1200 in Chartres, France. However, there are many labyrinth styles from which to choose (Kern, 2000).

Another option is to make a Circle of Life. For this option, when noted in the ceremonies below, the group makes four papers, one with North-Earth written on it, one with East-Air, one with South-Fire, and one with West-Water. A fifth paper is notated as Spirit. With the facilitator's guidance, the group comes up with words or phrases to put on each paper. This is in lieu of walking into the center of the labyrinth and can be done together. These are then placed in a moderately large circle, which the participant walks repeatedly until she feels she has completely incorporated what was written on the papers. She would then sit in the center. After the ceremony she would then be allowed to take these papers home as a tool to re-connect her to the ceremony experience.

In terms of instruction for the facilitator who uses this option, whenever the labyrinth is presented or incorporated into the ceremony, this option may be substituted. This substitution includes any Shamanic journey that takes place within the labyrinth. If using the Circle of Life option, the Shamanic journey would take place with the participant in the center of the Circle of Life.

Chapter 3

The Shamanic Ceremonies

This chapter includes the six Shamanic Ceremonies and Journeys for six transitions in a woman's life: Birth of a Girl Child, Honoring Self and Fertility, Becoming an Adult Female, Negotiating the Mid-Life Transition, Menopause and Birth of the Crone, and finally, the Death of the Crone. They are complete ceremonies, ready for a facilitator or guide to implement as is. However, they can also be modified as needed or wished.

Please note that when reading the Shamanic Journeys, they are spoken texts. As such, punctuation and grammar are not meaningful. Rather, flow and pauses are. Three dots (…) mean there is a pause in the journey. A new paragraph also notes a pause, but a larger one, more like a savoring-of-the-moment pause.

The more pauses, the more the participant is afforded the opportunity to connect to the journey, so feel free to pause frequently. Also, even though it may be quick to read the text of a journey, speaking it occurs at a slow, meandering, relaxed pace; a pace where words may dangle and the energy slowly spirals around them, creating a new, unspoken sense or bridge, or passage. A door opens, and …

Birth of Girl Child

The Birth of a Girl Child

This ceremony may take place at any time after the birth of a daughter. It does not need to occur immediately, for at any time one can hold On High to the Universe, a daughter's entrance into the female world clan.

Preparation Meeting and Preparation Period

During the preliminary meeting, the mother will be given information about what will occur and what is required of her. The father is welcomed, so that he, from the beginning, respects the Divine female within his daughter, and her female-ness.

At this preparation meeting, the ceremony is reviewed. The request is made for healthy eating, drinking, and physical self-care for the two days prior to the actual ceremony. Any other female or individual who wishes to welcome the girl child into the female clan may be invited.

The assignment: all participants will be asked to spend some time in reflection about their hopes and dreams for the infant and to bring these reflections to the ceremony.

The Beginning of the Ceremony

Upon arrival, the guide will make sure that the parent/ parents and friends are physically comfortable and the baby's needs, as best can be known ahead of time, are met.

As stated above, you, as guide, will explain that for Shamans the elements of Earth, Air, Fire, and Water are associated with the compass directions. The pairing of element with direction varies by Shamanic tradition. For this ceremony the pairings of direction with element are North-Earth, East-Air, South-Fire, and West-Water, which is common to the Celtic Shaman tradition. Six colored candles are brought forward: brown or green, yellow, red, blue, white, and purple. A compass is placed in a central spot so that all may be aware of the compass directions. Either you or the participants set the candles in their correct locations, with the brown or green one being placed in the North location, the yellow one in the East, red in the South, blue in the West, and white and purple placed in the center. All sit.

You explain that there will be Shamanic InWorld journeys and the participants will be asked to relax, close their eyes, and visualize the words that you say. Express also, that not all people visualize, but rather some sense, some feel, and some just listen; making sure that the participants know that there is no right and wrong to their experiences.

White washcloths are handed out and the participants told that they will use them later. They are directed to put the washcloths on their laps.

The essential oils are diffused or incense lit, and the candles are lit, marking that the ceremony has begun, using the following text.

Shamanic Journey to Open the Ceremony: As you are breathing in a relaxed manner, begin slowing down

The Birth of a Girl Child

the pace of the day, of yourself, and your Being. We will begin by diffusing the essential oils that were chosen (or if incense is used, modify wording accordingly).

(Pause while this is task is completed.)

Now we are going to light the ceremonial candles, and as we do so, we are opening our world here, to the Inner Realms and beginning to bring that energy here to us. We will do that by opening the directional-North, East, South, West-and elemental energies-Earth, Air, Fire, and Water, symbolizing that opening with the lighting of the candles. Are we ready? (If all affirm, continue.)

Again breathe slowly; and find yourself in a Central Area InWorld. There is a compass there and around you see the directions of North, East, South, and West. In each direction you will be seeing or sensing scenery, as I describe it.

First, we face to the North, and move towards the element of Earth. All around us is Earth. Mountains, rocks, canyons. A valley, with lush grass. A cave up ahead. Smell the Earth smells. Grass, trees, mud. We open our ceremony space to this energy and let it flow into this realm, like opening a giant curtain. We gently fling it open and the energy pours in to our ceremonial space. We light the green/brown candle, symbolizing this opening. And breathe in the Earth energy. (Either you or a participant lights the candle, with the others observing.)

Breathe slowly again; step back InWorld. And now we face East. To the element of Air. We open the curtains and we step into the Air. A light wind blows. Birds fly. Leaves blow. A wind storm you see furiously blowing in the distance. The crispness of spring. Like clothes on a clothesline lightly blowing in the breeze. And we invite the Air energy into this plane; lighting the yellow candle to symbolize the flow of Air energy to our realm. (Light candle.)

And now we open to the South, to the element of Fire. As we open these curtains we feel Fire as Summer, full Sun. Hot. But not desperately so. Fire in a fire pit. With Fire energy dancing on the licks of the flames. Bask in the power of the Fire energy. Creativity. Volcano in the distance, birthing itself. The invisible waviness above a fire, all around us here; without heat, just the energy. Open to it fully and we invite it into our plane, lighting the red candle to symbolize its presence. (Light candle.)

Breathe slowly. And now to the West, to the element of Water. The curtains open and we see a pool of water, the sun setting on the ocean in the distance. A river. Rain. Water is all around. We invite this element, and light the blue candle to symbolize its presence here. (Light candle.)

Return to the Inner Realms, breathing slowly. And now we turn back to the Central area where we began, *leaving all of the curtains open to allow the flow of the energy to continue. We breathe it all in. Looking North at Earth, then East at Air, South at Fire, and West at Water. What is left is Spirit, and we open to that. The Divine. Our Spirits. As we relax our Beings, and allow that to open, our energy flows out, mingles with the elemental energy, and the Divine. Both the Male Divine, the God-head, the Sun, as well as the female Divine, <u>our</u> Divine. The Moon, the goddess energy. Female energy. We invite the presence of Spirit and Higher powers to the ceremony and light the purple and white candles to symbolize this invitation. (Light candles.)*

We breathe in all we have opened to, allow the presence of all, even though we now open our eyes. We allow all of the energy to remain with us...we open our eyes, but remain open to All.

The Ceremony Proper

All will then proceed to discuss their hopes, dreams, and wishes for the girl child. As part of the discussion, emphasis will be placed upon her being a female and all that this role entails.

After talking at length about this, each participant will then be instructed to write their hopes and wishes for the baby on papers that are given to them, using waterproof ink. The leader will also keep a written copy of the statements to be used later in the ceremony.

A bowl with water is then brought out, put on the floor, and the participants are asked to sit in a circle around it. A brief Shamanic Journey on these hopes and wishes is done with the participants, with a focus on the thoughts and feelings of the parent(s). All participants follow along with the parent(s) in the journey.

Shamanic Journey on Hopes and Wishes for the Girl Child: Begin breathing in a relaxed manner, letting go of any thoughts that may pop into your head. Just know that thoughts will come, it is our nature. When they do, you will become aware of them, acknowledge that they are there, and just let them bubble up and away. Do not get down on yourself for it is a normal experience. So breathe in a relaxed manner. Letting the thoughts go as they arise.

Think back to the birth of your daughter, and even before her birth, all the hopes, and wishes, and dreams that you had for her. For her birth, for the family, for her growing up. For her life.

We talked about much of them, and more may come to any of you as you are sitting here in this relaxed state. In fact, if one comes to you, and it is of such impor-tance that you want it included, please state it and I will write it down.

Be with those times that you thought of your daugh-ter. ... and now sit with the feelings of her girl-ness;

The Birth of a Girl Child

her female-ness. Her being a part of the Divine female. And how you love this aspect of her.

And think of the statements that you have written. Fill her Being with those wishes. See her future with those dreams, and hopes, coming to fruition. (Pause)

And now, one by one, we will read the statements, and put them into the water basin. (The participants do this, and any additional ones that they want included, are added.)

Relax back into the moment, and see or sense or feel the water in the bowl, being infused with all that you wish for her; all that you hope for her; and all that you dream for her. ... And when you feel that it is time, come back to the here and now. Letting the water continue to hold all that is within it, as we continue.

After this phase is completed, physical comfort needs are again attended to for the adults and the baby. Then all relax in comfortable seating and are ready for the Shamanic Journey. They are told that the guide will take them InWorld and will be walking with them. The journey will include a brief InWorld cleansing and then the journey proper. For this InWorld cleansing, they will need the white washcloth that was handed out earlier, placed on their lap.

The Shamanic Ceremony Journey: Breathe in a natural and relaxed manner. Breathe in ... out ... in ... out. Remember thoughts may come; just let them go.

Breathe in. Out. Find yourself walking along a brook. I am walking with you and you are carrying your daughter. ... We are walking alongside the slow moving brook.

It bubbles, and slowly flows amongst the stones. As we walk, you feel every cell, and all of your body processes, slowly beginning to reset to the pace of the flow of the brook. And through you, your daughter also slows. ... To a comfortable, peaceful pace.

Up ahead there is a very shallow area, about 2 inches deep, with a nice bed of sand. We step in and feel the water. Feel the sand. It is a comfortable temperature.

As we breathe in, the bottom of our feet open, and up through our feet flows Water energy. Water energy is very cleansing and soothing and it cleanses us as it flows upwards. ... We breathe out, and toxins, and dust of the day, which is just the energetic residues that are created from normal life, flow out. ... We breathe in again, and the Water energy spirals and swirls higher ... and breathe out, the toxins and dust of the day, flow out down the brook. ... One more time in and the Water energy flows up to the top of your head ... and out, residues flow down the brook.

As you breathe the Water energy in and out slowly; and as it spirals within your Being, cleansing as it goes, you pick up the white washcloth from this realm. Back InWorld, you reach it down and soak it in the water of the brook. You walk to the shore and sit beneath a tree that is on the shoreline, with roots going right into the water. You lean with your back against the majestic tree, allowing your legs and feet to join with the tree roots, energetically connecting to the water you were just in.

As you lean back into the tree, you touch your forehead with the washcloth, both InWorld and in this realm, cleansing your 3rd Eye, so that you may discern all that you 'see' intuitively, discern with wisdom. ... You wash your eyes so that you may see clearly in the Outer Realms. ... You wash your ears, so that you may hear without your ego interfering. ... You wash your mouth, so that you might speak clearly, kindly, and with love. ... And, you wash your heart, so that you feel and give love unconditionally.

You reflect on this girl child, and all send spiritual cleansing to her with your heart. And in the Inner Realms, you wash her body with the washcloth so she is energetically clean for her ceremony.

We are now cleansed and ready to walk further. ... We step out of the water and head West. West is the direction of the element of Water. And Water is female. In the Heavens above, in the West, is the Moon. Also female. So we head to the female; the Divine female; the mystical Divine. ...

After some time, we arrive in the West. There is a beautiful sunset; with dusk arriving. It is fall-like in the air, with some crispness, although not uncomfortable. But all around you sense Water. Ocean waves, the sea. A river flowing into the sea. Rain on the horizon. Dampness. A healing pool next to you.

Water is all around. Open yourself to feel it. … Breathe it in. … The Water energy mingles with your Being, which is mostly water. Flowing through you also is Female energy. The Female Water energy. … Positive, solid but flowing delicately, but sturdily. You feel the positive nature of the mystical Divine female.

And you look up. To the Universe, in the West. You see the Moon. … You feel the Moon. Creamy, silky flow of Moon energy fills you. Subtle but strong. Pure.

And you see a Moon beam which is like a set of steps that goes right up to the Heavens from here. I turn, you turn, and we start up the steps. … We walk up, as the steps spiral up to the Heavens. One by one, till we arrive.

And here it is, glorious. Wondrous. The Heavens. We see four female Beings. The Moon Beings. One representing the Full Moon, one the Dark Moon, one for the First Quarter and one for the Last Quarter Moon. They bid us to come to stand in front of them, and we walk over.

The Birth of a Girl Child

They motion us to stand, in front of the place where they are moving to sit. They ask what we are requesting, and I respond, "We come to register this girl child." They see her, stand to look at her, and ask her name. I turn to you and say, "You may state her full name." (The mother states the infant's name.) As you do so, one writes it in the large book that is there.

Another one asks what is hoped for her, and I respond. (I read the hopes.) ... She turns to you and asks, "Is this so?" You say, "Yes." (Pause) She acknowledges and you see another one has been writing the list of hopes next to your daughter's name.

The Dark Moon Being says, "It is time; to acknowledge her birth and fill her with your hopes for her." The Full Moon Being says, "and to fill her with her birthright; the mystical, Divine female. Of which we represent."

They motion you to a basin. You look around and it is beautiful here. You carry your daughter over and the first Moon Being, the Dark Moon Being, anoints her and whispers a message to you, about your daughter. ... Tell me what she says, and I will write it down so you remember.

The First Quarter Being comes forward, and anoints her, also telling you a message. Tell me.

The Full Moon Being does the same, tell me.

And then the Last Quarter Being does so, tell me.

After they are done, they stand around us, and signal for the Heavens to open, and suddenly, from the Universe, from the Male Divine, flows pure white Light. ... Love ... Compassion ... Unconditional connectedness ... Purity ... Divine ... All ... Completion. It all flows through us.

Then the Moon Beings open the Female Moon energy to fill us. Creamy ... Silky ... Female love ... Completion ... Mother love. Deep Unconditional Love.

Sit with all of this energy; feel it. Fill yourself with it. And through you, your daughter fills.

Your daughter is registered, filled with the Divine Male energy and the Divine Female energy, as well as your hopes, and your dreams. She is ready to Be. The light slows and fades. We thank the Universe, the Moon Beings, and walk back the way we came. Back to the brook and out.

The guide asks the parent(s) and participants to become comfortable and journal a bit about their experience. The parent(s) are handed back the paper with both the wishes they have for their daughter and the messages from the Moon Beings, which the guide has been writing down. They are also given the water from the bowl, along with the statements still in the water. As a group, talk about what can be done with the water, i.e., put it all into a blender and then make ice cubes out of it to be used at a later date for another ritual that they may wish to do.

Participants are then provided with dye and other art materials in order to personalize their washcloths that were used in the spiritual cleansing ritual. This way they have an outward sign of the ceremony that they have just completed.

The End of the Ceremony

After they are done writing, reflecting, and decorating their washcloths, they process the entire day, and then do the closing, and extinguish the candles.

Shamanic Journey to Close the Ceremony: As we opened the InWorld curtains and lit the candles, so must we close the curtains and extinguish the oils/ incense and candles. Breathe in a relaxed manner and we find ourselves back in the Central Area, like the center of the compass. We breathe in all that we have done today. All the feelings, sensations, experiences. ... We look North at the element of Earth, release the energy and close the curtain. We extinguish the brown/green candle to symbolize this closing. (Extinguish candle.)

We look East, at the element of Air, and let go of that energy, closing the curtain, and extinguishing the yellow candle. (Extinguish candle.)

We look to the South, to the element of Fire, and release that energy, closing the curtain, and extinguishing the red candle. (Extinguish candle.) And we look to the West, to the element of Water, releasing that energy, with which we have spent much time today. Fondly letting it go, closing the curtain and extinguishing the blue candle. (Extinguish candle.)

We are left with Spirit. The Divine. Male and Female. Proud of Female. Deeply connecting to that energy. We will allow that connection to continue as we extinguish both the white and purple candles. We allow the Divine to flow within us. We hold our Beings On High and remain deeply connected to the Heavens, the Universe. Breathe this in as we begin to return to this day. This realm. This plane. And we open our eyes to the ordinary. Knowing where we have been and what we have done and what we can do. (Extinguish candles.)

Honoring Self and Fertility

The Honoring of Self and Fertility

This ceremony is planned for a girl who has started menstruating and is about 12-13 years of age. The focus of the ceremony is to help the girl understand that her body is sacred, that she is sacred, and that she is part of a long line of Divine females, including angels, goddesses, saints, and Mother Earth. As such, she is expected to protect and nourish her body, to love it and care for it, and to do the same for her Soul. Invited to this ceremony are any females with whom she wishes to share the day.

Preparation Meeting and Preparation Period

Present at her preparation meeting are the girl and her mother, or a mother surrogate. Prior to attending the meeting, the mother will be asked to have a thorough, age-appropriate discussion of female sexuality with the girl. At the preparation meeting the facilitator will ask the girl to talk about her first menstruation and how it fits into overall female sexuality. This is done for two reasons. First, to make sure there was no negative experience with the first menstruation, and second, to make sure the girl is at ease with and respectful of basic femaleness.

At this preparation meeting, the ceremony is reviewed. The request is made for healthy eating, drinking, and physical self-care for the two days prior to the actual ceremony. The mother and girl are asked who they would like to participate in the ceremony and told of the following assignment.

The assignment: The mother is requested to bring a list of names of the females in the family of origin, and each attendee, including the young girl, is requested to bring a list of at least three females who have been influential to them and why or how they have been influential. They can be family, alive, dead, historical, or biblical. What is important is the connection of female to female, past, present, and future.

The Beginning of the Ceremony

Upon arrival, all participants' physical needs will be met and everyone made comfortable. The overall flow of the ceremony will be explained.

As stated above, you, as guide, will explain that for Shamans the elements of Earth, Air, Fire, and Water are associated with the compass directions. The pairing of element with direction varies by Shamanic tradition. For this ceremony the pairings of direction with element are North-Earth, East-Air, South-Fire, and West-Water, which is common to the Celtic Shaman tradition. Six colored candles are brought forward: brown or green, yellow, red, blue, white, and purple. A compass is placed in a central spot so that all may be aware of the compass directions. Either you or the participants set the candles in their correct locations, with the brown or green one being placed in the North location, the yellow one in the East, red in the South, blue in the West, and white and purple placed in the center. All sit.

The Honoring of Self and Fertility

You explain that there will be Shamanic InWorld journeys and the participants will be asked to relax, close their eyes, and visualize the words that you say. Express also, that not all people visualize, but rather some sense, some feel, and some just listen; making sure that the participants know that there is no right and wrong to their experiences.

White washcloths are handed out and the participants told that they will use them later. They are directed to put the washcloths on their laps.

When everyone is comfortable and any questions answered, lights will be dimmed, the ceremony will begin with the essential oils or incense being lit, and then the candle lighting within the following Shamanic journey.

Shamanic Journey to Open the Ceremony: As you are breathing in a relaxed manner, begin slowing down the pace of the day, of yourself, and your Being. We will begin by diffusing the essential oils that were chosen (or if incense is used, modify wording accordingly).

(Pause while this is task is completed.)

Now we are going to light the ceremonial candles, and as we do so, we are opening our world here, to the Inner Realms and beginning to bring that energy here to us. We will do that by opening the directional-North, East, South, West-and elemental energies-Earth, Air, Fire, and Water, symbolizing that opening with the lighting of the candles. Are we ready? (If all affirm, continue.)

Again breathe slowly; and find yourself in a Central Area InWorld. There is a compass there and around you see the directions of North, East, South, and West. In each direction you will be seeing or sensing scenery, as I describe it.

First, we face to the North, and move towards the element of Earth. All around us is Earth. Mountains, rocks, canyons. A valley, with lush grass. A cave up ahead. Smell the Earth smells. Grass, trees, mud. We open our ceremony space to this energy and let it flow into this realm, like opening a giant curtain. We gently fling it open and the energy pours in to our ceremonial space. We light the green/brown candle, symbolizing this opening. And breathe in the Earth energy. (Either you or a participant lights the candle, with the others observing.)

Breathe slowly again; step back InWorld. And now we face East. To the element of Air. We open the curtains and we step into the Air. A light wind blows. Birds fly. Leaves blow. A wind storm you see furiously blowing in the distance. The crispness of spring. Like clothes on a clothesline lightly blowing in the breeze. And we invite the Air energy into this plane; lighting the yellow candle to symbolize the flow of Air energy to our realm. (Light candle.)

And now we open to the South, to the element of Fire. As we open these curtains we feel Fire as Summer, full

The Honoring of Self and Fertility

Sun. Hot. But not desperately so. Fire in a fire pit. With Fire energy dancing on the licks of the flames. Bask in the power of the Fire energy. Creativity. Volcano in the distance, birthing itself. The invisible waviness above a fire, all around us here; without heat, just the energy. Open to it fully and we invite it into our plane, lighting the red candle to symbolize its presence. (Light candle.)

Breathe slowly. And now to the West, to the element of Water. The curtains open and we see a pool of water, the sun setting on the ocean in the distance. A river. Rain. Water is all around. We invite this element, and light the blue candle to symbolize its presence here. (Light candle.)

Return to the Inner Realms, breathing slowly. And now we turn back to the Central area where we began, leaving all of the curtains open to allow the flow of the energy to continue. We breathe it all in. Looking North at Earth, then East at Air, South at Fire, and West at Water. What is left is Spirit, and we open to that. The Divine. Our Spirits. As we relax our Beings, and allow that to open, our energy flows out, mingles with the elemental energy, and the Divine. Both the Male Divine, the God-head, the Sun, as well as the female Divine, <u>our</u> Divine. The Moon, the goddess energy. Female energy. We invite the presence of Spirit and Higher powers to the ceremony and light the purple and white candles to symbolize this invitation. (Light candles.)

We breathe in all we have opened to, allow the presence of all, even though we now open our eyes. We allow all of the energy to remain with us…we open our eyes, but remain open to All.

The Ceremony Proper

A discussion will then ensue of the adolescent's female history, her female family history, and females in general. This is where each participant will talk about the females on their lists. Throughout the discussion, the general theme will be about honoring Self, honoring females, and honoring fertility. After the discussion, a short break may be taken. Afterward, all will go on the Shamanic Journey, although the main participant will be the girl.

The Shamanic Ceremony Journey: Begin breathing in a relaxed manner, letting go of any thoughts that may pop into your head. Just know that thoughts will come; it is our nature. When they do, you will become aware of them, acknowledge that they are there, and just let them bubble up and away. Do not get down on yourself, for it is a normal experience. So breathe in, in a relaxed manner. Letting the thoughts go as they arise. Breathe in … out … in … out. And find yourself walking along a brook. I am walking with you. … We are walking alongside the slow moving brook.

The Honoring of Self and Fertility

It bubbles, and slowly flows amongst the stones. As we walk, you feel every cell, and every one of your body processes, slowly beginning to reset to the pace of the flow of the brook. … To a comfortable, peaceful pace.

Up ahead there is a very shallow area, about 2 inches deep, with a nice bed of sand. We step in and feel the water. Feel the sand. It is a comfortable temperature.

As we breathe in, the bottom of our feet open, and up through our feet flows Water energy. Water energy is very cleansing and soothing and it cleanses us as it flows upwards. … We breathe out, and toxins, and dust of the day, which is just the energetic residues that are created from normal life, flow out. … We breathe in again, and the Water energy spirals and swirls higher … and breathe out, the toxins and dust of the day, flow out down the brook. … One more time in and the Water energy flows up to the top of your head … and out, residues flow down the brook.

As you breathe the Water energy in and out slowly; and as it spirals within your Being, cleansing as it goes, you pick up the white washcloth from this realm. Back InWorld, you reach it down and soak it in the water of the brook. You walk to the shore and sit beneath a tree that is on the shoreline, with roots going right into the water. You lean with your back against the majestic tree, allowing your legs and feet to join with the tree roots, energetically connecting to the water you were just in.

As you lean back into the tree, you touch your forehead with the washcloth, both InWorld and in this realm, cleansing your 3rd Eye, so that you may discern all that you 'see' intuitively, discern with wisdom. ... You wash your eyes so that you may see clearly in the Outer Realms. ... You wash your ears, so that you may hear without your ego interfering. ... You wash your mouth, so that you might speak clearly, kindly, and with love. ... And, you wash your heart, so that you feel and give love unconditionally.

We are now cleansed and ready to walk further. ... We step out of the water and head West. West is the direction of the element of Water. And Water is female. In the Heavens above, in the West, is the Moon. Also female. So we head to the female; the Divine female; the mystical Divine. ...

After some time, we arrive in the West. There is a beautiful sunset; with dusk arriving. It is fall-like in the air, with some crispness, although not uncomfortable. But all around you sense Water. Ocean waves, the sea. A river flowing into the sea. Rain on the horizon. Dampness. A healing pool next to you.

Water is all around. Open yourself to feel it. ... Breathe it in. ... The Water energy mingles with your Being, which is mostly water. Flowing through you also is Female energy. The Female Water energy. ... Positive, solid but flowing delicately, but sturdily. You feel the positive nature of the mystical Divine female.

And you look up. To the Universe, in the West. You see the Moon. ... You feel the Moon. Creamy, silky flow of Moon energy fills you. Subtle but strong. Pure.

And you see a Moon beam that is like a set of steps that go right up to the Heavens from here. I turn, you turn, and we start up the steps. ... We walk up, as the steps spiral up to the Heavens. One by one, till we arrive.

And here it is, glorious. Wondrous. The Heavens. We see four female Beings. The Moon Beings. One representing the Full Moon, one the Dark Moon, and one for the First Quarter and one for the Last Quarter Moon. They bid us to come to stand in front of them, and we walk over.

They are beautiful. All dressed in white. A little transparent, for they are not of this world.

They ask the one who is to be initiated to step forward. They call for her. ... (Say her name.) ... "Be not afraid," says the Dark Moon Being. She herself steps forward, and holds her hand out to you.

"So you are she who comes for a re-birth. To let go of being a little girl; to become a young woman. Oh, you

can still be silly or play, but you are also a woman now. And this is what we shall initiate. You will step into your rightful place as female Divine. With a long line of women who have stepped forward; who have lived as females. Both in your family, on Earth, and the Divine. If you turn and look back, you will see that there are too many women to count. And if you look forward, you will see that there are many more to come. You have heard some of their stories, as she points back to the women who have been in line. And some day a girl will be standing right where you are, and your story will be one of the ones told. I feel already that you are going to be important. Now though, you are to walk with me."

We watch as the two of you walk to the other three Moon Beings. The three of them are sitting in comfy chairs and there is even a chair for you. You sit there, with them.

The Dark Moon Being says, "I represent the letting go of old ways of being, and the rebirth into a new way of being. That is why I am leading today. What we are going to do, is one by one, we are each going to tell you something very important about being a female. And you are to tell your guide, so she can write it down for you."

The first one to tell you an important aspect of being a female is the Dark Moon Being. She leans over to

The Honoring of Self and Fertility

you and whispers something into your ear. Now you may not hear in the normal Outer World way. Rather, you may just sense a phrase, or know one, or feel one. However you do, tell me what she has spoken to you so that I may write it down. (Pause to write.)

Next, the First Quarter Moon Being comes over to you, greets you, and then whispers to you. As you know it, tell me so that I might write it down. (Pause to write.)

The Full Moon Being then comes over and does the same. (Pause to write). And finally, the Last Quarter Moon Being comes over and speaks to you. (Pause to write.)

"I now am going to let the First Quarter Moon Being lead the next part" says the Dark Moon Being.

She steps forward and says, "I represent the beginning of growth of the Moon, as it has come out of the dark time of the month. My job is to have the Moon Beings tell you, and then you tell your guide, a truth. Now a Truth is something that is important and true no matter when or where you live. It is just a Truth, like, be kind to others. It is true no matter what. But these truths are not just random, they are important to you, as female. As we tell you these Truths, you say them out loud so that your guide can write them down."

(Each one does so in turn, as above, and they are spoken to be written down. The guide directs this phase,

inviting the Moon Beings over, and asking the participant what was said, then inviting the next Moon Being and so on.)

"My job is done, and now it is time for the Full Moon Being to lead."

She steps forward. "I represent Fullness, creativity, and power. My job is to have each Being tell you a strength that you have."

(Each does so and they are written down. The guide directs this phase, inviting the Moon Beings over, and asking the participant what was said, then inviting the next Moon Being and so on.)

The Last Quarter Moon Being steps forward and says, "I represent a slowing, and beginnings of reflection. My job is to direct each of us to tell you something you need to think about or be aware of. Like, you need to know this, or you need to know that."

(Each does in turn and they are written down. The guide directs this phase, inviting the Moon Beings over, and asking the participant what was said, then inviting the next Moon Being and so on.)

When they have all finished the Full Moon Being steps forward and asks, "Do you have any questions, because you have just heard a lot of information." (Give the young woman time to ask anything she wishes. This

The Honoring of Self and Fertility

may be for clarification or more information. Help her ask if she does want to speak with the Moon Beings.)

The Full Moon Being then turns to the rest of us and says for everyone to step forward. And circle around (girl's name). When everyone is ready, she does a signal and immediately the Heavens open ... and suddenly, from the Universe, from the Male Divine, flows pure white Light. Love ... compassion ... unconditional connectedness ... Purity ... Divine ... All ... Completion. It flows through us.

Then the Moon Beings open the Female Moon energy to fill us. Creamy ... silky ... Female love ... Completion ... Mother love. Deep Unconditional Love.

We are filled with both the Divine Male and Female.

"(Girl's name) is ready to Be; to be a part of the Divine Female." The light slows and fades. We thank the Universe, the Moon Beings, and walk back the way we came. Back to the brook and out.

Paper and pencils are handed out to journal and/or draw the experience, after which the journey is processed. The participants are directed to sit and, with art supplies provided, draw or write notes to the young girl that are pertinent to the experience, to the focus of the ceremony, or to the girl in general.

The next part of the ceremony involves walking a labyrinth. For questions regarding use of a labyrinth, please see the section on use of spiritual tools in Chapter 2, and an alternative option to the use of a labyrinth.

Based upon the experiences to this point, the group as a whole comes up with a mantra for the girl to use during her walk to the center of the labyrinth. She walks by herself with the other women watching and supporting. Once in the center, the art work and notes the women worked on just prior are brought out to her, as are the materials brought to the ceremony by all, and the notes from the journey on what the Moon Beings told her. She reads all of the information. She then opens an envelope with an assignment inside. Here she is asked to write a letter to the mystical Divine female, thanking her for her femaleness, for her menses, and for her Being-ness. She is asked to describe what she has learned that day and how she can incorporate it into her life.

While the young woman has been working in the labyrinth center or with an alternative option, the others work together on a letter to her, dedicating their support to her as a new young woman as she continues her walk through life. They then, as a group, walk the labyrinth into the center to be with the girl, using a mantra that they have deemed appropriate. This mantra is repeated out loud during the entire walk to the center. Or, in the alternative option, the group comes to her, sitting on Spirit. There she reads to them what she has written. And they read what they have written to her.

Once completed, the group goes to a comfortable place. They are provided with dye and other art materials in order to personalize their washcloth that was used in the spiritual cleansing ritual. This way they have an outward sign of the ceremony that they have just completed.

All of the work will then be placed into a suitable container which the girl will take home with her. The women, who have come with her, are requested to keep in contact with her, continuing to support her development into a young woman.

The End of the Ceremony

After they are done writing, reflecting, and decorating their washcloths, they process the entire day, and then do the closing, and extinguish the candles.

Shamanic Journey to Close the Ceremony: As we opened the InWorld curtains and lit the candles, so must we close the curtains and extinguish the oils/incense and candles.

Breathe in a relaxed manner and we find ourselves back in the Central Area, like the center of the compass. We breathe in all that we have done today. All the feelings, sensations, experiences. ... We look North at the element of Earth, release the energy and close the curtain. We extinguish the brown/green candle to symbolize this closing. (Extinguish candle.)

We look East, at the element of Air, and let go of that energy, closing the curtain, and extinguishing the yellow candle. (Extinguish candle.)

We look to the South, to the element of Fire, and release that energy, closing the curtain, and extinguishing the red candle. (Extinguish candle.)

And we look to the West, to the element of Water, releasing that energy, with which we have spent much time today. Fondly letting it go, closing the curtain and extinguishing the blue candle. (Extinguish candle.)

We are left with Spirit. The Divine. Male and Female. Proud of Female. Deeply connecting to that energy. We will allow that connection to continue as we extinguish both the white and purple candles. We allow the Divine to flow within us. We hold our Beings On High and remain deeply connected to the Heavens, the Universe. Breathe this in as we begin to return to this day. This realm. This plane. And we open our eyes to the ordinary. Knowing where we have been and what we have done and what we can do. (Extinguish candles.)

Becoming an Adult Woman

The Becoming of an Adult Woman

Just when does one become an adult? In our culture, it is not really clear when an adolescent actually becomes an adult. We know that the age of majority, becoming an adult, legally is age 18. But that magic number does not necessarily mean that a young person is ready to be an adult. We have no ceremony, no ritual with which our culture uses to help the adolescent take that step into adulthood.

The following ceremony is meant to provide the adolescent, who has decided that she is ready, with a ceremony to help her, her peers, and her family, recognize that she is ready to make, or has made, the transition. The young woman who participates can be any age after age 18.

Preparation Meeting and Preparation Period

In the preliminary meeting the topic of transitioning into adulthood is addressed with her and her mother, or a significant female adult. She is questioned about her readiness to step beyond adolescence into young adulthood; into young female adulthood. Is she ready to take her place with other women who have stepped into the adult female?

At this preparation meeting, the ceremony is reviewed. The request is made for healthy eating, drinking, and physical self-care for the two days prior to the actual ceremony.

After a successful discussion, she and her mother will be directed to bring any female over age 18, whom she would like to have as an active participant in her ceremony. The women are asked to bring drums or related items if they own them.

Assignment: The young woman is given a homework assignment of drawing or writing about leaving childhood to become a woman. This is to be done in at least two mediums, such as an essay and drawing, or she may write a poem and make a collage.

The Beginning of the Ceremony

The attendees will arrive, meet and greet each other, questions asked and answered and, after getting comfortable, you will present a general discussion of the ceremony.

As stated above, you, as guide, will explain that for Shamans the elements of Earth, Air, Fire, and Water are associated with the compass directions. The pairing of element with direction varies by Shamanic tradition. For this ceremony the pairings of direction with element are North-Earth, East-Air, South-Fire, and West-Water, which is common to the Celtic Shaman tradition. Six colored candles are brought forward: brown or green, yellow, red, blue, white, and purple. A compass is placed in a central spot so that all may be aware of the compass directions. Either you or the participants set the candles in their correct locations, with the brown or green one being placed in the North location, the yellow one in the East, red in the South,

The Becoming of an Adult Woman

blue in the West, and white and purple placed in the center. All sit.

You explain that there will be Shamanic InWorld journeys and the participants will be asked to relax, close their eyes, and visualize the words that you say. Express also, that not all people visualize, but rather some sense, some feel, and some just listen; making sure that the participants know that there is no right and wrong to their experiences.

White washcloths are handed out and the participants told that they will use them later. They are directed to put the washcloths on their laps.

The ceremony begins with the lighting of the incense or diffusing of the essential oils, and the candles being lit, as detailed in the following Shamanic Journey.

Shamanic Journey to Open the Ceremony: As you are breathing in a relaxed manner, begin slowing down the pace of the day, of yourself, and your Being. We will begin by diffusing the essential oils that were chosen (or if incense is used, modify wording accordingly).

(Pause while this is task is completed.)

Now we are going to light the ceremonial candles, and as we do so, we are opening our world here, to the Inner Realms and beginning to bring that energy here to us. We will do that by opening the directional-North, East, South, West-and elemental energies-Earth, Air, Fire, and Water, symbolizing that opening with the lighting of the candles. Are we ready? (If all affirm, continue.)

Again breathe slowly; and find yourself in a Central Area InWorld. There is a compass there and around you see the directions of North, East, South, and West. In each direction you will be seeing or sensing scenery, as I describe it.

First, we face to the North, and move towards the element of Earth. All around us is Earth. Mountains, rocks, canyons. A valley, with lush grass. A cave up ahead. Smell the Earth smells. Grass, trees, mud. We open our ceremony space to this energy and let it flow into this realm, like opening a giant curtain. We gently fling it open and the energy pours in to our ceremonial space. We light the green/brown candle, symbolizing this opening. And breathe in the Earth energy. (Either you or a participant lights the candle, with the others observing.)

Breathe slowly again; step back InWorld. And now we face East. To the element of Air. We open the curtains and we step into the Air. A light wind blows. Birds fly. Leaves blow. A wind storm you see furiously blowing in the distance. The crispness of spring. Like clothes on a clothesline lightly blowing in the breeze. And we invite the Air energy into this plane; lighting the yellow candle to symbolize the flow of Air energy to our realm. (Light candle.)

And now we open to the South, to the element of Fire. As we open these curtains we feel Fire as Summer, full Sun. Hot. But not desperately so. Fire in a fire pit. With Fire energy dancing on the licks of the flames. Bask in the power of the Fire energy. Creativity. Volcano in the distance, birthing itself. The invisible waviness above a fire, all around us here; without heat, just the energy. Open to it fully and we invite it into our plane, lighting the red candle to symbolize its presence. (Light candle.)

Breathe slowly. And now to the West, to the element of Water. The curtains open and we see a pool of water, the sun setting on the ocean in the distance. A river. Rain. Water is all around. We invite this element, and light the blue candle to symbolize its presence here. (Light candle.)

Return to the Inner Realms, breathing slowly. And now we turn back to the Central area where we began, leaving all of the curtains open to allow the flow of the energy to continue. We breathe it all in. Looking North at Earth, then East at Air, South at Fire, and West at Water. What is left is Spirit, and we open to that. The Divine. Our Spirits. As we relax our Beings, and allow that to open, our energy flows out, mingles with the elemental energy, and the Divine. Both the Male Divine, the God-head, the Sun, as well as the female Divine, <u>our</u> Divine. The Moon, the goddess energy. Female energy. We invite the presence of Spirit and Higher powers to *the ceremony and light the purple and white candles to symbolize this invitation. (Light candles.)*

We breathe in all we have opened to, allow the presence of all, even though we now open our eyes. We allow all of the energy to remain with us...we open our eyes, but remain open to All.

The Ceremony Proper

The participants are asked to discuss their own transition to adulthood; the good, the bad, and the ugly: the choices they made, the ones they regret, and the ones they felt positive about, as well as how all those choices affected their lives. The young woman can also talk about the choices she has made to this point in her life, including those she regrets. This entire discussion takes place in a non-judgmental way. When this discussion ends, and everybody is comfortable, the Shamanic Journey begins. All go on the Shamanic Journey, but the main participant is the young woman.

The Shamanic Ceremony Journey: Begin breathing in a relaxed manner, letting go of any thoughts that may pop into your head. Just know that thoughts will come, it is our nature. When they do, you will become aware of them, acknowledge that they are there, and just let them bubble up and away. Do not get down on yourself for it is a normal experience. So breathe in a relaxed manner. Letting the thoughts go as they arise. Breathe in ... out ... in ... out. And find yourself walking along a brook. I am walking with you. ... We are walking alongside the slow moving brook.

It bubbles, and slowly flows amongst the stones. As we walk, you feel every cell, and every one of your body processes, slowing, beginning to reset to the pace of the flow of the brook. ... To a comfortable, peaceful pace.

Up ahead there is a very shallow area, about 2 inches deep, with a nice bed of sand. We step in and feel the water. Feel the sand. It is a comfortable temperature.

As we breathe in, the bottom of our feet open, and up through our feet flows Water energy. Water energy is very cleansing and soothing and it cleanses us as it flows upwards. ... We breathe out, and toxins, and dust of the day, which is just the energetic residues that are created from normal life, flow out. ... We breathe in again, and the Water energy spirals and swirls higher ... and breathe out, the toxins and dust of the day, flow out down the brook. ... One more time in and the Water energy flows up to the top of your head ... and out, residues flow down the brook.

As you breathe the Water energy in and out slowly; and as it spirals within your Being, cleansing as it goes, you pick up the white washcloth from this realm. Back

InWorld, you reach it down and soak it in the water of the brook. You walk to the shore and sit beneath a tree that is on the shoreline, with roots going right into the water. You lean with your back against the majestic tree, allowing your legs and feet to join with the tree roots, energetically connecting to the water you were just in.

As you lean back into the tree, you touch your forehead with the washcloth, both InWorld and in this realm, cleansing your 3rd Eye, so that you may discern all that you 'see' intuitively, discern with wisdom. ... You wash your eyes so that you may see clearly in the Outer Realms. ... You wash your ears, so that you may hear without your ego interfering. ... You wash your mouth, so that you might speak clearly, kindly, and with love. ... And, you wash your heart, so that you feel and give love unconditionally.

We are now cleansed and ready to walk further. ... We step out of the water and head West. West is the direction of the element of Water. And Water is female. In the Heavens above, in the West, is the Moon. Also female. So we head to the female; the Divine Female; the mystical Divine. ...

After some time, we arrive in the West. There is a beautiful sunset; with dusk arriving. It is fall-like in the air, with some crispness, although not uncomfortable. But all around you sense Water. Ocean waves, the sea. A river flowing into the sea. Rain on the horizon. Dampness. A healing pool next to you.

Water is all around. Open yourself to feel it. ... Breathe it in. ... The Water energy mingles with your being, which is mostly water. Flowing through you also is Female energy. The Female Water energy. ... Positive, solid but flowing delicately, but sturdily. You feel the positive nature of the mystical Divine Female.

And you look up. To the Universe, in the West. You see the Moon. ... You feel the Moon. Creamy, silky flow of Moon energy fills you. Subtle but strong. Pure.

And you see a Moon beam that is like a set of steps that go right up to the Heavens from here. I turn, you turn, and we start up the steps. ... We walk up, as the steps spiral up to the Heavens. One by one, till we arrive.

And here it is, glorious. Wondrous. The Heavens. We see four female Beings. The Moon Beings. One representing the Full Moon, one the Dark Moon, and one for the First Quarter and one for the Last Quarter Moon. They bid us to come to stand in front of them, and we walk over.

They are beautiful. All dressed in white. A little transparent, for they are not of this world. They ask the one who is to be initiated to step forward.

They call for you. … (Say her name).

The Being that represents the Dark Moon asks you to step forth. And you do, with me by your side. She walks us forward, asking me to stop … and then walks you to the center, between all of them.

You look at all of them. You had never thought you would see such beauty … such purity.

Swirling invisibly around you is the Moon energy. You feel the sweetness of it, the creaminess. … It flows gently around you. … You realize that you had lost track of what they were saying, and apologize, saying this is all new for you.

They are genuinely caring, and say that it is fine. They ask you if you are ready to be initiated into the Clan of the Moon. To Adult Womanhood. And you respond yes, that you are.

And they ask, how you know it is time; that your maturity has grown enough. You ponder for a moment, and tell them, how you know you are ready. (The guide turns to the young woman and asks her to tell them.)

They look at each other and affirm your response. They say, you may step forward.

They open their circle, letting you in, and in front of you is a white crystal pallet. A place to lie down upon that is pure white crystal. ... They point that you are to lay there. And you do.

The Dark Moon Being says that you are about to begin the transition. And that they will, one by one, work on your Inner Being, helping it heal, let go of old ways of being, and open to the new ways of being that are necessary for joining the Clan; to truly become Woman.

The Being that represents the First Quarter steps forward and she, with her hands about an inch above your body, scans your body surface.

Every once in a while she stops and takes either a plant, a crystal, a stone, a gem, or some other item, out of a basket that is sitting there. She then places that item on that part of your body.

You are very aware of what she is doing, even if it does not make sense. After she is done, signal me by lifting your finger. ... (Finger lifts)

The Full Moon Being steps forth, radiating the Moon Light around her. She does the same thing. Scanning your body and taking items out of the basket, placing them on you in various places. When she is done, lift your finger to let me know. (Finger lifts)

The Being representing the Last Quarter steps forth and repeats what the others have done before her. (Finger lifts)

And finally the Being representing the Dark Moon steps forward. She studies what they have done. ... Scans and adds a couple more items. ... And then takes out a bucket of deep dark purple salve.

She paints it all over your Being. ... She says, "Do not worry, this salve is of the Universe" as she continues to paint the salve on you.

After she has painted the salve on you, they circle you again and start spinning around you a filament cocoon. ... Until you are almost totally encapsulated into it; all but your face.

You know that in the life of a butterfly, this means the butterfly is in a cocoon, and is about to emerge, and you somehow know that this is true with you. That this is about your birth, as Woman.

They take you to the Full Moon and place you there on a pallet. You can feel yourself absorbing the pure white Light of the Moon.

You slowly feel female angels gracefully flying gently around you, helping to cut the filament. As they do so they are whispering loving words to you; words of welcome.

Listen to their words. ... As you slowly become free.

And finally you are. Free.

You stand tall; gracefully, in a beautiful white iridescent robe. You breathe, and take it all in for a moment.

And you confidently walk back down to the Moon Beings and tell them you have become a woman. ... And are ready to join them, and the others.

They ask you to come and sit with them, and each one, one at a time, tells you something you need to know about being a woman. As they do so, tell me so that I can write it down for you so that you can remember.

First the Dark Moon Being tells you (tell me so I can write it down)

Then the First Quarter Being (write it down).

Then the Full Moon Being (write it down).

And finally, the Last Quarter Being (write it down).

When they are done we thank them and come back, joining the others who have been waiting and come out, back to the brook, and back out.

After this Shamanic Journey and a quick break, the women get their drums or other music/sound makers and head out to the labyrinth. Please see the section on the use of spiritual tools in Chapter 2, for information about labyrinths, and an alternative option that can be used instead.

75

The young woman is instructed on how to do a labyrinth and a mantra is chosen for her by the group. The drumming begins, and she walks in to the center of the labyrinth, repeating the mantra. In the center she finds instructions that she will be taken on another journey, as well as paper and pencil to take notes. The other women continue to drum as she does the journey. Once all are ready, you go to the center and read the following journey to the participant.

Shamanic Journey in the Center of the Labyrinth: When you are comfortable, find yourself walking along the brook and up ahead you find a group of women. They are the Council of Wise Women. Make a note of how many there are, and how they are dressed. (Pause while she does so. At any time she needs more directedness to complete these tasks; you may direct the journey more.)

You stand in front of them, newly Woman of the Clan, and stand with your arms open wide to the Heavens, baring your Soul to the Divine. You then face them. They congratulate you on your achievement. And one by one, they will tell you an inner strength that you have and a wisdom statement, some statement of Truth about Life. Write them down as they tell you. (Pause while she does so.)

When they are done, thank them, and then walk back to the brook. There will be a tree, and sitting, leaning against the tree is like a fairy princess sort of being. She is magical and loving, and represents the innocence that we all need to nurture in ourselves. She will talk to you about what you have experienced.

You may ask her anything and she will answer. Write down notes about your conversation. When you are done, she will tell you, your mantra for the way out. Write it down. And walk out. (Pause until she is ready to walk out.)

When the young female walks out of the labyrinth, she is greeted as Woman. The others are then invited to walk the labyrinth with the same instructions in the center. Other participants read the journey to those who arrive in the center. Drumming will continue until all have walked and returned. After this segment there will be a short snack break.

After the break, the participants are sent to journal and/or draw with art supplies provided. They will be instructed to write about their experiences and to write the young woman a letter welcoming her to womanhood, and how they, a solitary woman within a group of women, will support her in her continuing maturational process. The young woman will be asked to process her day, including all that was told to her by the Moon Beings and by the Wise Women.

After everyone has written, all of the information is shared and written materials gathered for the young woman to take with her so that she may refer to all that occurred this day whenever she wants.

Additionally, they are provided with dye and other art materials in order to personalize their washcloth that was used in the spiritual cleansing ritual. This way they have an outward sign of the ceremony that they have just completed.

The End of the Ceremony

After they are done writing, reflecting, and decorating their washcloths, they process the entire day, and then do the closing, and extinguish the candles.

Shamanic Journey to Close the Ceremony: As we opened the InWorld curtains and lit the candles, so must we close the curtains and extinguish the oils/ incense and candles. Breathe in a relaxed manner and we find ourselves back in the Central Area, like the center of the compass. We breathe in all that we have done today. All the feelings, sensations, experiences. ... We look North at the element of Earth, release the energy and close the curtain. We extinguish the brown/green candle to symbolize this closing. (Extinguish candle.)

We look East, at the element of Air, and let go of that energy, closing the curtain, and extinguishing the yellow candle. (Extinguish candle.)

We look to the South, to the element of Fire, and release that energy, closing the curtain, and extinguishing the red candle. (Extinguish candle.)

And we look to the West, to the element of Water, releasing that energy, with which we have spent much time today. Fondly letting it go, closing the curtain and extinguishing the blue candle. (Extinguish candle.)

We are left with Spirit. The Divine. Male and Female. Proud of Female. Deeply connecting to that energy. We will allow that connection to continue as we extinguish both the white and purple candles. We allow the Divine to flow within us. We hold our Beings On High and remain deeply connected to the Heavens, the Universe. Breathe this in as we begin to return to this day. This realm. This plane. And we open our eyes to the ordinary. Knowing where we have been and what we have done and what we can do. (Extinguish candles.)

Negotiating the Mid-Life Transition

Somewhere in the middle adult years, the focus of life changes from other-centeredness to self-centeredness. Typically, the female has spent her whole life focusing on boyfriends, then spouse, then children, and so on. At some point, she may feel as though she gave too much or that she has focused nothing on herself. This can often lead to disillusionment and depression as well as unhealthy attempts to rectify the situation, often by focusing on Self almost exclusively. This ceremony serves to ease that transition, make sense of it, and help facilitate a healthy shift in life focus.

Preparation Meeting and Preparation Period

The preliminary meeting will focus on an interview about any angst or unhappiness in the woman's life, where she is at, where she has come from, and where she sees herself going. If where she sees herself going in the future brings her unhappiness of some sort and thus, if this end point needs to be adjusted, then that is discussed as well. The whole transition is normalized as a natural part of individual development, with a healthy transition being the focused end result.

The woman is asked to take exceptional self-care in the two days prior to the ceremony. She is also told that she can bring as many female friends or family members as she wishes.

The assignment: The woman will be asked specifically to journal in certain categories. It will be her developmental timeline. She will be asked to reflect upon and note feelings and events which were important to her emotionally, physically, and spiritually, as related to this life transition, during each five years of her life. Additionally she will be asked to reflect on and note feelings on events that she sees in her future, if she makes the changes that she knows she needs to make.

She will be asked to make the appointment for her ceremony once she has completed this life assessment and will be directed to bring the paper work with her.

The Beginning of the Ceremony

On the day of the ceremony, the guide will speak privately and in depth with the woman about her life history journal. There will be a strong focus on how she perceives her future. She will be asked to spend some contemplative time reflecting on all that she has done in preparation and the discussion that she just had with the guide. Art supplies will be provided for her if she is so inclined to use them.

Once the other women have arrived, they will be asked if they have any questions, the plan for the day reviewed, and they will be made physically comfortable.

As stated above, you, as guide, will explain that for Shamans the elements of Earth, Air, Fire, and Water are associated with the compass directions. The pairing of element with direction varies by Shamanic tradition. For this ceremony the pairings of direction with element are North-Earth, East-Air, South-Fire, and

West-Water, which is common to the Celtic Shaman tradition. Six colored candles are brought forward: brown or green, yellow, red, blue, white, and purple. A compass is placed in a central spot so that all may be aware of the compass directions. Either you or the participants set the candles in their correct locations, with the brown or green one being placed in the North location, the yellow one in the East, red in the South, blue in the West, and white and purple placed in the center. All sit.

You explain that there will be Shamanic InWorld journeys and the participants will be asked to relax, close their eyes, and visualize the words that you say. Express also, that not all people visualize, but rather some sense, some feel, and some just listen; making sure that the participants know that there is no right and wrong to their experiences.

White washcloths are handed out and the participants told that they will use them later. They are directed to put the washcloths on their laps.

The opening will begin with the diffusing of essential oils or incense; and candle lighting, as detailed in the following Shamanic Journey.

Shamanic Journey to Open the Ceremony: As you are breathing in a relaxed manner, begin slowing down the pace of the day, of yourself, and your Being. We will begin by diffusing the essential oils that were chosen (or if incense is used, modify wording accordingly).

(Pause while this is task is completed.)

Mother Maiden Crone

Now we are going to light the ceremonial candles, and as we do so, we are opening our world here, to the Inner Realms and beginning to bring that energy here to us. We will do that by opening the directional-North, East, South, West-and elemental energies-Earth, Air, Fire, and Water, symbolizing that opening with the lighting of the candles. Are we ready? (If all affirm, continue.)

Again breathe slowly; and find yourself in a Central Area InWorld. There is a compass there and around you see the directions of North, East, South, and West. In each direction you will be seeing or sensing scenery, as I describe it.

First, we face to the North, and move towards the element of Earth. All around us is Earth. Mountains, rocks, canyons. A valley, with lush grass. A cave up ahead. Smell the Earth smells. Grass, trees, mud. We open our ceremony space to this energy and let it flow into this realm, like opening a giant curtain. We gently fling it open and the energy pours in to our ceremonial space. We light the green/brown candle, symbolizing this opening. And breathe in the Earth energy. (Either you or a participant lights the candle, with the others observing.)

Breathe slowly again; step back InWorld. And now we face East. To the element of Air. We open the curtains and we step into the Air. A light wind blows. Birds fly.

Leaves blow. A wind storm you see furiously blowing in the distance. The crispness of spring. Like clothes on a clothesline lightly blowing in the breeze. And we invite the Air energy into this plane; lighting the yellow candle to symbolize the flow of Air energy to our realm. (Light candle.)

And now we open to the South, to the element of Fire. As we open these curtains we feel Fire as Summer, full Sun. Hot. But not desperately so. Fire in a fire pit. With Fire energy dancing on the licks of the flames. Bask in the power of the Fire energy. Creativity. Volcano in the distance, birthing itself. The invisible waviness above a fire, all around us here; without heat, just the energy. Open to it fully and we invite it into our plane, lighting the red candle to symbolize its presence. (Light candle.)

Breathe slowly. And now to the West, to the element of Water. The curtains open and we see a pool of water, the sun setting on the ocean in the distance. A river. Rain. Water is all around. We invite this element, and light the blue candle to symbolize its presence here. (Light candle.)

Return to the Inner Realms, breathing slowly. And now we turn back to the Central area where we began, leaving all of the curtains open to allow the flow of the energy to continue. We breathe it all in. Looking North at Earth, then East at Air, South at Fire, and West at

Water. What is left is Spirit, and we open to that. The Divine. Our Spirits. As we relax our Beings, and allow that to open, our energy flows out, mingles with the elemental energy, and the Divine. Both the Male Divine, the God-head, the Sun, as well as the female Divine, our Divine. The Moon, the goddess energy. Female energy. We invite the presence of Spirit and Higher powers to the ceremony and light the purple and white candles to symbolize this invitation. (Light candles.)

We breathe in all we have opened to, allow the presence of all, even though we now open our eyes. We allow all of the energy to remain with us...we open our eyes, but remain open to All.

The Ceremony Proper

The group will discuss the same topics the woman had written about and shared with the guide in the above section. When all are ready, the Shamanic Journey will begin. All go on the Shamanic Journey, but the main participant is the woman.

The Shamanic Ceremony Journey (throughout the journey, information ascertained from her journaling will be incorporated): Begin breathing in a relaxed manner, letting go of any thoughts that may pop into your head. Just know that thoughts will come, it is our nature. When they do, you will become aware of them, acknowledge that they are there, and just let them bubble up and away. Do not get down on yourself for it is a normal experience. So breathe in a relaxed manner. Letting the thoughts go as they arise. Breathe in ... out ... in ... out. And find yourself walking along a brook. I am walking with you. ... We are walking alongside the slow moving brook.

It bubbles, and slowly flows amongst the stones. As we walk, you feel every cell, and every one of your body processes, slowing, beginning to reset to the pace of the flow of the brook. ... To a comfortable, peaceful pace.

Up ahead there is a very shallow area, about 2 inches deep, with a nice bed of sand. We step in and feel the water. Feel the sand. It is a comfortable temperature.

As we breathe in, the bottom of our feet open, and up through our feet flows Water energy. Water energy is very cleansing and soothing and it cleanses us as it flows upwards. ... We breathe out, and toxins, and dust of the day, which is just the energetic residues that are created from normal life, flow out. ... We breathe in again, and the Water energy spirals and swirls higher ... and breathe out, the toxins and dust of the day, flow out down the brook. ... One more time in and the Water energy flows up to the top of your head ... and out, residues flow down the brook.

As you breathe the Water energy in and out slowly; and as it spirals within your Being, cleansing as it goes, you pick up the white washcloth from this realm. Back InWorld, you reach it down and soak it in the water of the brook. You walk to the shore and sit beneath a tree that is on the shoreline, with roots going right into the water. You lean with your back against the majestic tree, allowing your legs and feet to join with the tree roots, energetically connecting to the water you were just in.

As you lean back into the tree, you touch your forehead with the washcloth, both InWorld and in this realm, cleansing your 3ʳᵈ Eye, so that you may discern all that you 'see' intuitively, discern with wisdom. ... You wash your eyes so that you may see clearly in the Outer Realms. ... You wash your ears, so that you may hear without your ego interfering. ... You wash your mouth, so that you might speak clearly, kindly, and with love. ... And, you wash your heart, so that you feel and give love unconditionally.

We are now cleansed and ready to walk further.

We step out of the water and you notice that we are now clothed in white robes, but of strong material, for we are going on a long journey.

We walk together, side by side, to the Center, where we see 2 steeds. ... Mine knows me and comes right up to me. The other comes a little more shyly. We both mount our steeds. And, holding on, we bound off to the North. (If there are others present, they are invited to join us on their steeds, riding behind us.)

We ride hard, and long, North-ward ... finally arriving at the outer reaches, where we turn left.

We are riding a large circle, large as the World, large as the Universe, a circle counter-clockwise. North, to West, to South, to East, to North, and around again. Each complete circle is a year in time and we are riding time backwards...to your beginning.

We circle and circle, endlessly it seems. We tire, but the steeds know what they must do, and keep running hard. ... Tirelessly. ... Round and round. ... Till finally, after it seems like forever, they begin to slow.

To a walk and then to a stop. ... They let us off at the edge of a grove in the North and we enter. Walking forward till we come to a clearing.

There is a fire going in the center, and a tender, tending to it. ... We walk up to the fire, warm our hands and greet the tender. He says, "Hey," and points to the shadows, saying, "You want him."

Out steps our guide, from the shadows. He sits down, and motions for us to sit down as well, waving the tender away, so we are all alone. ...

He says, "I know why you are here, but I want her to say it" pointing to you. You tell him what you are here for. I then add, "She is coming for her transition. She needs to let the old her die to her old ways of being, die to them; and a new her, with new ways of being, to be born anew."

He nods his head at the both of us. Takes out a pipe and stuffs the bowl with dried leaves that will allow you to let go, even more, of the present. He hands it to you, and lights it up. ... You breathe in the smoke and feel a floating sensation come over you.

He says, "You are ready" and he asks me to step back.

"I want you to tell me," he says," your biggest regret about your life." You do. (I tell her that it can be said totally InWorld, and thus silent, or she can say it out loud. If it is said InWorld, I tell her to tell me when she is done).

"And I want you to tell me what you are proudest of" (stated out loud, or signaled when done).

"I want you to tell me the biggest way you want to be different and how that will look to others" (stated out loud, or signaled when done).

"I want you to see you, being like that...and as you do so, I want you to lie on this pallet." You comply, even

though you can still see you, who you will be, in the future.

As you lay there, he sprinkles Light dust on you. ... That is, dust, made from Light particles.

As they land on you, they do something magical. ... They make you glow in every little place they land. ... And you begin to feel the glowing till you are like a light bulb.... And you let go...becoming Light energy. (Big pause)

Suddenly you realize you are within the 'you' in the future. ... And you feel her. ... You feel You. ... What you would feel like. The good and the bad. ... Feel it. Memorize it. And return to the pallet.

The Healer says to rise and you do, you thank him, and come to me, and we mount our steeds. Riding clockwise this time ... back to our time ... and then beyond. ... Till we arrive at the 'you' in the future, that you saw.

There 'you' are again. This time in all your glory. We quietly dismount and go sit and watch 'you.'

I say, "Tell me about her." (Gather info and ad lib from here based on the info—with part of the purpose being that she connect to a healthier her.)

She, the 'you' in the future, notices us finally; we must have made a little too much noise. But she is ok with it.

Mother Maiden Crone

She comes over, recognizing you. And says she wants to talk to you. She wants to tell you how she is differ- ent and how it changed her life. Tell me her words; the words she says to you. (You might help her ask the future her questions about her life.)

You tell her that you are going to walk a labyrinth and that you need a mantra to use to walk the path in. Ask her if she can tell you the most important wisdom that she learned and we will make it into a mantra.

Thank her and we return....we mount our steeds, ride counter clockwise back to this time. Dismount and walk along the brook to the here and now.

After a break, and reflection with the group, all go to the labyrinth. Please see the section on the use of spiri- tual tools in Chapter 2, for information about labyrinths and alternative option to use instead.

The guide explains to the woman that walking into the labyrinth (or an alternative option) is for letting go. Each step of the way, she is to think about the aspects of her past that she wrote of, then say the mantra, and imagine herself in the future. She is to do this repeat- edly until she reaches the center. Once there, the guide will join her and take her on another journey.

Shamanic Journey in the Center of the Labyrinth: Find yourself walking by the brook, and, after a bit, we turn West again.

Remember, West is the direction of the element of Water. And Water is female. In the Heavens above, in the West, is the Moon. Also female. So we head to the female; the Divine Female; the mystical Divine.

And we arrive in the West. There is a beautiful sunset; with dusk arriving. It is fall-like in the air, with some crispness, although not uncomfortable. But all around you sense Water. Ocean waves, the sea. A river flowing into the sea. Rain on the horizon. Dampness. A healing pool next to you. Water is all around. ... Open yourself to feel it. ... Breathe it in.

The Water energy mingles with your Being, which is mostly water. ... Flowing through you also is Female energy. ... The Female Water energy. ... Positive. ... Solid, but flowing delicately, but sturdily. ... You feel the positive nature of the mystical Divine Female. ... I point to the Moon above and then to a Moon beam that is coming right down to us, and when we look closely, we see that it has formed itself into spiral steps up to the Moon.

We walk them. Spiraling around till we arrive. ... At the Full Moon. We hear, "Can the woman step forward?"

You do. Immediately there is pure Moon light all around you. And you open yourself to absorb it. ... Creamy ... Silky ... Loving ... Pure ... Wondrous. Unconditional Love.

Mother Maiden Crone

The 'you' in the future steps out to face you. ... The two of you walk towards each other, and she says, "I invite you to become me. ... To feel me. ... To know me. ... I allow you to step into all aspects of my Being and own them for yourself. All that you want to be. It is balanced. It is not Self centered, nor Other centered. It is balanced."

She continues, "After you step in, you can absorb the balance; it is my gift to you. And then you can step out. And keep all that you absorbed." ... "I am ready" she says.

So you step forward and merge with her. The healthy you in the future. ... You feel it. The health. The completeness. The balance. The giving and the receiving. The dependence and independence. ... And you realize, that is what it is all about. Balance. Seeing each situation, from both ways of seeing it, and then making a choice how to respond. But ultimately, it all has to balance. For that is the way. ... You are amazed by what you feel and what you learned. (Give time for her to be in the experience fully.)

A mantra comes to you for the way out. Each step on the way out, alternate feeling the balance with saying the mantra.

After she returns, she is asked to spend some time in reflection and journaling or drawing her experiences and thoughts. The other women are invited to walk the labyrinth. Since they completed the main journey, another participant may read to them the journey for the center of the labyrinth. When they return, all spend time discussing the day.

Additionally, they are provided with dye and other art materials in order to personalize their washcloth that was used in the spiritual cleansing ritual. This way they have an outward sign of the ceremony that they have just completed.

The End of the Ceremony

After they are done writing, reflecting, and decorating their washcloths, they process the entire day, and then do the closing, and extinguish the candles.

Shamanic Journey to Close the Ceremony: As we opened the InWorld curtains and lit the candles, so must we close the curtains and extinguish the oils/incense and candles. Breathe in a relaxed manner and we find ourselves back in the Central Area, like the center of the compass. We breathe in all that we have done today. All the feelings, sensations, experiences. ... We look North at the element of Earth, release the energy and close the curtain. We extinguish the brown/green candle to symbolize this closing. (Extinguish candle.)

We look East, at the element of Air, and let go of that energy, closing the curtain, and extinguishing the yellow candle. (Extinguish candle.)

We look to the South, to the element of Fire, and release that energy, closing the curtain, and extinguishing the red candle. (Extinguish candle.)

And we look to the West, to the element of Water, releasing that energy, with which we have spent much time today. Fondly letting it go, closing the curtain and extinguishing the blue candle. (Extinguish candle.)

We are left with Spirit. The Divine. Male and Female. Proud of Female. Deeply connecting to that energy. We will allow that connection to continue as we extinguish both the white and purple candles. We allow the Divine to flow within us. We hold our Beings On High and remain deeply connected to the Heavens, the Universe. Breathe this in as we begin to return to this day. This realm. This plane. And we open our eyes to the ordinary. Knowing where we have been and what we have done and what we can do. (Extinguish candles.)

Menopause, the Birth of the Crone

Menopause, the Birth of the Crone

The transition through peri-menopause to menopause can take years and can, but not always, be a time of major physiological and emotional changes. Those changes, often held in silence, can cause a woman tremendous angst. Sometimes it is laughed off, with statements about hot flashes, but there is much more to it than that. The emotional aspects alone can be overwhelming.

With a ceremony, the whole transition can be rejoiced. This ceremony can be done at any time during or after the transition to Crone.

Preparation Meeting and Preparation Period

During the preliminary meeting, a rough assessment will be made of what stage of this transition the woman is in as well as a discussion about how it is affecting her.

Assignment: The woman will be asked to read at least one book on the subject of menopause so that she has some understanding about the changes happening to her and her body. She will also be asked to journal who she felt she was before the transition began, during the transition (depending on where she is in the progression of it), and where she has come to, or hopes to come to when the transition is complete.

Once these two assignments are done, she may participate in the ceremony. She may also invite other women to participate with her and celebrate afterward. All participants will be asked to eat, drink, and sleep healthily during the two days prior to the ceremony.

The Beginning of the Ceremony

Upon arrival, the overall structure of the ceremony will be discussed and questions asked and answered. The participant and guide will privately talk about her journaling and then, the group, if there is one, will have a discussion during which each woman states where they are at in the menopause transition and how they have felt about the process. After the women's physical needs are met and all are comfortable, the ceremony will begin.

As stated above, you, as guide, will explain that for Shamans the elements of Earth, Air, Fire, and Water are associated with the compass directions. The pairing of element with direction varies by Shamanic tradition. For this ceremony the pairings of direction with element are North-Earth, East-Air, South-Fire, and West-Water, which is common to the Celtic Shaman tradition. Six colored candles are brought forward: brown or green, yellow, red, blue, white, and purple. A compass is placed in a central spot so that all may be aware of the compass directions. Either you or the participants set the candles in their correct locations, with the brown or green one being placed in the North location, the yellow one in the East, red in the South, blue in the West, and white and purple placed in the center. All sit.

You explain that there will be Shamanic InWorld journeys and the participants will be asked to relax, close their eyes, and visualize the words that you say. Express also, that not all people visualize, but rather some sense, some feel, and some just listen; making sure that the participants know that there is no right and wrong to their experiences.

White washcloths are handed out and the participants told that they will use them later. They are directed to put the washcloths on their laps.

The essential oils or incense are lit, and then the candles are lit as detailed in the following Shamanic Journey.

Shamanic Journey to Open the Ceremony: As you are breathing in a relaxed manner, begin slowing down the pace of the day, of yourself, and your Being. We will begin by diffusing the essential oils that were chosen (or if incense is used, modify wording accordingly).

(Pause while this is task is completed.)

Now we are going to light the ceremonial candles, and as we do so, we are opening our world here, to the Inner Realms and beginning to bring that energy here to us. We will do that by opening the directional-North, East, South, West-and elemental energies-Earth, Air, Fire, and Water, symbolizing that opening with the lighting of the candles. Are we ready? (If all affirm, continue.)

Again breathe slowly; and find yourself in a Central Area InWorld. There is a compass there and around you see the directions of North, East, South, and West. In each direction you will be seeing or sensing scenery, as I describe it.

First, we face to the North, and move towards the element of Earth. All around us is Earth. Mountains, rocks, canyons. A valley, with lush grass. A cave up ahead. Smell the Earth smells. Grass, trees, mud. We open our ceremony space to this energy and let it flow into this realm, like opening a giant curtain. We gently fling it open and the energy pours in to our ceremonial space. We light the green/brown candle, symbolizing this opening. And breathe in the Earth energy. (Either you or a participant lights the candle, with the others observing.)

Breathe slowly again; step back InWorld. And now we face East. To the element of Air. We open the curtains and we step into the Air. A light wind blows. Birds fly. Leaves blow. A wind storm you see furiously blowing in the distance. The crispness of spring. Like clothes on a clothesline lightly blowing in the breeze. And we invite the Air energy into this plane; lighting the yellow candle to symbolize the flow of Air energy to our realm. (Light candle.)

And now we open to the South, to the element of Fire. As we open these curtains we feel Fire as Summer, full Sun. Hot. But not desperately so. Fire in a fire pit. With Fire energy dancing on the licks of the flames. Bask in the power of the Fire energy. Creativity. Volcano in the distance, birthing itself. The invisible waviness above a fire, all around us here; without heat, just the energy.

Open to it fully and we invite it into our plane, lighting the red candle to symbolize its presence. (Light candle.)

Breathe slowly. And now to the West, to the element of Water. The curtains open and we see a pool of water, the sun setting on the ocean in the distance. A river. Rain. Water is all around. We invite this element, and light the blue candle to symbolize its presence here. (Light candle.)

Return to the Inner Realms, breathing slowly. And now we turn back to the Central area where we began, leaving all of the curtains open to allow the flow of the energy to continue. We breathe it all in. Looking North at Earth, then East at Air, South at Fire, and West at Water. What is left is Spirit, and we open to that. The Divine. Our Spirits. As we relax our Beings, and allow that to open, our energy flows out, mingles with the elemental energy, and the Divine. Both the Male Divine, the God-head, the Sun, as well as the female Divine, <u>our</u> Divine. The Moon, the goddess energy. Female energy. We invite the presence of Spirit and Higher powers to the ceremony and light the purple and white candles to symbolize this invitation. (Light candles.)

We breathe in all we have opened to, allow the presence of all, even though we now open our eyes. We allow all of the energy to remain with us...we open our eyes, but remain open to All.

The Ceremony Proper

If there are enough in attendance, they will sit in a circle around the woman and the guide. If not, they will sit with the woman. All go on the Shamanic Journey, but the main participant is the woman.

The Shamanic Ceremony Journey: Begin breathing in a relaxed manner, letting go of any thoughts that may pop into your head. Just know that thoughts will come, it is our nature. When they do, you will become aware of them, acknowledge that they are there, and just let them bubble up and away. Do not get down on yourself for it is a normal experience. So breathe in a relaxed manner. Letting the thoughts go as they arise. in ... out ... in ... out. And find yourself walking along a brook. I am walking with you. ... We are walking alongside the slow moving brook.

It bubbles, and slowly flows amongst the stones. As we walk, you feel every cell, and every one of your body processes, slowing, beginning to reset to the pace of the flow of the brook. ... To a comfortable, peaceful pace.

Up ahead there is a very shallow area, about 2 inches deep, with a nice bed of sand. We step in and feel the water. Feel the sand. It is a comfortable temperature.

As we breathe in, the bottom of our feet open, and up through our feet flows Water energy. Water energy is very cleansing and soothing and it cleanses us as it flows upwards. ... We breathe out, and toxins, and dust of the day, which is just the energetic residues that are created from normal life, flow out. ... We breathe in again, and the Water energy spirals and swirls higher ... and breathe out, the toxins and dust of the day, flow out down the brook. ... One more time in and the Water energy flows up to the top of your head ... and out, residues flow down the brook.

As you breathe the Water energy in and out slowly; and as it spirals within your Being, cleansing as it goes, you pick up the white washcloth from this realm. Back InWorld, you reach it down and soak it in the water of the brook. You walk to the shore and sit beneath a tree that is on the shoreline, with roots going right into the water. You lean with your back against the majestic tree, allowing your legs and feet to join with the tree roots, energetically connecting to the water you were just in.

As you lean back into the tree, you touch your fore-head with the washcloth, both InWorld and in this realm, cleansing your 3rd Eye, so that you may discern all that you 'see' intuitively, discern with wisdom. ... You wash your eyes so that you may see clearly in the Outer Realms. ... You wash your ears, so that you may hear without your ego interfering. ... You wash your mouth, so that you might speak clearly, kindly, and with love. ... And, you wash your heart, so that you feel and give love unconditionally.

We are now cleansed and ready to walk further. ... We step out of the water and head West. West is the direction of the element of Water. And Water is female. In the Heavens above, in the West, is the Moon. Also female. So we head to the female; the Divine Female; the mystical Divine. ...

After some time, we arrive in the West. There is a beautiful sunset; with dusk arriving. It is fall-like in the air, with some crispness, although not uncomfortable. But all around you, you sense Water. Ocean waves, the sea. A river flowing into the sea. Rain on the horizon. Dampness. A healing pool next to you.

Water is all around. Open yourself to feel it. ... Breathe it in. ... The Water energy mingles with your Being, which is mostly water. Flowing through you also is Female energy. The Female Water energy. ... Positive, solid but flowing delicately, but sturdily. You feel the positive nature of the mystical Divine Female.

And you look up. To the Universe, in the West. See the Moon. ... Feel the Moon. Creamy, silky flow of energy fills you. Subtle but strong. Pure. Unconditional Love.

Suddenly you sense a presence and turn. It is a female Being and she says, she will take us up to the Moon Beings because they are ready for us.

She points to a spiral staircase and we walk to it. When we look up, from the base of the steps, it seems like there is no ending to it. ... She begins to walk up it. And we follow.

I understand that part of the purpose of the steps is that, as we go, it is an ordeal, and you are to also let go of the old you and all that this means to you. And that also is an ordeal.

I talk to you about this, and tell you that each step we make, you will think of who you were and begin to shed it so that you may step into a new role, one of Wise Woman, or Crone.

We walk and you do this. Images pop up into your head, and you let them go. ... They remain part of your history but letting them go will allow a new you to emerge.

Step step step (Give the woman plenty of time for the process).

Finally we reach the top. ... You are amazed to see that we are in the Universe, on the Moon. And there are four Moon Beings there. ... One for each main Moon phase: Dark, Full, First Quarter, and Last Quarter.

The Dark Moon Being steps forward. She represents death to an old way of being and rebirth to a new way of being. ... She greets you, saying "Welcome. I am so glad that you have come." The others come forward and circle you; I step back.

They put their hands, their palms, on the top of your head; your connection to the Divine.

The Full Moon Being gives a signal and the Heavens open up. ... Pure Light flows down through their hands and into you, through the top of your head, your Crown energy center. ... It is like their hands have attracted the Light and brought more of it into your Crown than would have naturally occurred.

It feels powerful. ... Male ... Pure ... Love ... Sun.

The Light of the Universe fills you instantly. ... And then it stops. The Full Moon Being gives another signal, and Moon Light starts flowing into you, in the same way.

This Light energy feels very different. It is more subtle. ... Creamy ... Smooth ... Female ... No less powerful, but very different ... Female Love ... Purity.

It fills you as well. And it stops.

The four Moon Beings then take their hands off of your head and form a circle around you, holding hands. ... They all signal together and the male Sun Light energy and the female Moon Light energy begin to spiral within you.

Intertwining ... Co-mingling ... Powerfully.

The Full Moon Being says, "Now is the time to open to both the male and female aspects of the Divine, of the Universe, of the Light. You are to be balanced, equal, with both Male and Female energies. We did that with the Heavens and now it is time to open to both in the Under World, deep within the Earth." We thank them and walk back down the steps, quicker than we had come up them.

When we get to the bottom we walk out of the West. To a Central Area. You then feel roots growing from your feet to the Earth ... Deeper and deeper they go.

As they drill through the Earth you feel yourself flowing down these roots. Deeper and deeper ... Ending finally at a Central Area deep within the core of the Earth; in the Under World, the realm of ancestors and totems.

You feel Earth, smell Earth, and open to Earth, to Mother Earth. ... The female aspect of the Earth's energy. Commonly felt as female, hence the 'Mother' Earth of some form, in many cultures. Open to that energy. ... Swirling within you. See it manifesting as growth, growth of seeds, plants, the forests; and the cycle of life...plants dying to be transformed to new life. Deep groundedness ... Feel the female aspect of this.

You feel directed to walk to the caves to the North of you; in the North. ... And so you head that way. ... One seems different and feels like it is calling to you to

Mother Maiden Crone

enter. ... You make your way to it and you enter. As you enter, you begin to feel the depth of the Earth. ... You see a sprinkling of light around, and you are not sure if it comes from candles, or Under World stars, or fireflies...but you feel that something mystical lights your way.

You walk deeper, and hidden in the deep, is a pallet; made of deep dark onyx. You lie upon it, and immediately relax into a peaceful state.

A Deep Earth Being brings a basket of stones and crystals to place on any necessary energy centers...as she does so; you spiral deeper with the healing. ... (Give her time for this process.)

Each cycle of the spiral representing a letting go of the conceptions of Male on Earth. ... Father ... brother ... uncle ... boss. ... Letting go of any and all of the negativity for the negativity is of our earthly, or Outer Realm, and not of the Inner Realms. Let it all go so that you may enter the presence of the Deep Male more fully and more purely. (Long pause)

You finally arrive after much shedding...to a place that is deep ... powerful ... male ... rooted.

Open to the knowledge that the Male and Female energies are both very important. And within the Under World, along with the Earth Mother, there is a Deep

Male essence. Feel what this means to you. ... What images, feelings, sensations appear. ...

And, then you see Him ... in whatever form he materializes to you. A Being, a Bull. ... However he comes to you ... He is the power of the Earth's sun. He is the pure power. Maker of fossils. Of oil. Of diamonds. He is the pressure of the Earth. He has been lost to us, as has been, had been, the Earth Mother and goddess.

Feel the difference between the Deep Male energy and the Earth Mother energy. Together, they are One.

As you turn your head, you see both. ... Connect to both and feel whole ... complete ... the power ... the primal sexual energy ... the Bull and the Cow.

Oil. Diamonds. Magma. Fossils. Rock. Solid. Burning. Roots. Reaching down deep. Core. Let that Male energy flow up into your Being. Plants, seeds, growth, transformation, cycling of Life. Let that Female energy flow into your Being. The Deep Male and Earth Mother.

As this new connection percolates within you, I sit next to you and talk to you of the shift that is occurring (depending on where she is in the process). That with menopause, the female hormones have decreased or are mostly gone. And that opens you up to allow the Male energy within you, and the balance of Male and Female energy.

Only then can you be totally balanced. Only then can you be the Wise Woman, or Crone. "Welcome," I say. "Keep exploring the balance. The Unity." (Long pause)

When we are done, we walk back up to the Central Area. There is a tree, your tree. Your Inner Tree. Your Tree of Life.

You walk to it, and find you can step inside. As you do so you let yourself energetically flow out the top to the branches and to the Universe, opening up to both the Male and Female Light energies. The pure white Light of the male Divine, and the Sun, and the silky creamy Light of the female Divine, and the Moon.

These energies spiral down through you. As they do, your legs and feet flow down the roots and open to the Male and Female energy of the Earth. The Earth Mother, and the Deep Male. Those energies flow up and then comingle with the energy of the Heavens.

You sense a spiraling together like a maypole and the energies connect, merge, within you.

As you breathe in, all of the energy flows to the Heavens, and as you breathe out, it all together flows to the Earth. ... In and up ... out and down. ... Over and over.

Until you are at such peace and such balance that you let go, and become Nothing. No Self ... No structure. Just Nothingness.

You find you are flowing all through the Universe. ... Wonder ... Peace ... Purity. And all through the center of the Earth ... Bliss ... Quietness ... Power. ... Yin-yang. You no longer exist as Being, but rather as pure energy. ... Radiating ... Male ... Female. You understand the balance. You feel the balance. You want the balance.

Slowly you re-coalesce. Coming back to this plane of existence. Thankful for what you have learned.

From here, the Crone prepares to walk the labyrinth by first sitting and reflecting on the journey. Please see the section on spiritual tools in Chapter 2, for information on labyrinths and for an alternative option that can be used instead.

She is given a mantra, either by the guide or her friends, that is reflective of the Male-Female energy balance and becoming the Crone. She walks to the center of the labyrinth repeating that mantra. Once there, the guide joins her and takes her on a short journey.

Shamanic Journey in the Center of the Labyrinth: We find ourselves walking again by the brook, and then head to the West. To the healing pool that was there before. You de-clothe and slowly step in. You realize that this water is Moon water. And you absorb the energy fully.

As you lay in the pool, the heavens open up and the archangels begin to sing the tones of the universe.

First one archangel, singing one tone. ... Joined by another archangel singing another tone. ... And another ... And another ... Until the Universe is filled with the tones.

The tones swirl around you, increasing your vibration as the tones increase in vibration. You feel the intensity around you increasing.

Then the Earth opens up, and the tones begin down there. One tone at a time, deeply resonating with the tones that flow from the Universe.

These tones swirl around you. They are different. Less light. More deep power. Different. Equal.

You attend to the tones. And within them, you hear the female. ... The male. ... And you allow them to enter your being. Tuning you up.

And you once again let go ... becoming Nothing. I will walk away, and you may stay in this state of Nothingness. Of Peace ... Harmony ... Balance ... The balance of Male-Female. The integration of opposites. The Knowing. The Crone.

When you are done, and you may take whatever time you want, you will return to this plane with a new mantra to walk out with. Sit in peace and let the mantra come to you. Once you have the mantra, you may walk out of the labyrinth using it.

But you may stay as Nothingness as long as you wish. Flowing within the Universe and at the same time, flowing within the Earth. Holding All together as One. Peacefully.

While she is walking the others remain silent; holding her On High. When she returns, they, as a group or individually, may then walk the labyrinth with another participant reading the short journey in the center.

The Crone is asked to spend some quiet time journaling her experience and how she will integrate it into her life and her menopause transition. The others can journal as well. After some time of quiet, the experience is processed all together.

Additionally, the women are provided with dye and other art materials in order to personalize their washcloth that was used in the spiritual cleansing ritual. This way they have an outward sign of the ceremony that they have just completed.

The End of the Ceremony

After they are done writing, reflecting, and decorating their washcloths, they process the entire day, and then do the closing, and extinguish the candles.

Shamanic Journey to Close the Ceremony: As we opened the InWorld curtains and lit the candles, so must we close the curtains and extinguish the oils/incense and candles. Breathe in a relaxed manner and we find our-

selves back in the Central Area, like the center of the compass. We breathe in all that we have done today. All the feelings, sensations, experiences. ... We look North at the element of Earth, release the energy and close the curtain. We extinguish the brown/green candle to symbolize this closing. (Extinguish candle.)

We look East, at the element of Air, and let go of that energy, closing the curtain, and extinguishing the yellow candle. (Extinguish candle.)

We look to the South, to the element of Fire, and release that energy, closing the curtain, and extinguishing the red candle. (Extinguish candle.)

And we look to the West, to the element of Water, releasing that energy, with which we have spent much time today. Fondly letting it go, closing the curtain and extinguishing the blue candle. (Extinguish candle.)

We are left with Spirit. The Divine. Male and Female. Proud of Female. Deeply connecting to that energy. We will allow that connection to continue as we extinguish both the white and purple candles. We allow the Divine to flow within us. We hold our Beings On High and remain deeply connected to the Heavens, the Universe. Breathe this in as we begin to return to this day. This realm. This plane. And we open our eyes to the ordinary. Knowing where we have been and what we have done and what we can do. (Extinguish candles.)

The Death of the Crone

This is the inevitable final life transition. This ceremony can be done for any deceased woman; however, an added focus on wisdom is present for a woman in the sunset of her years, the Crone. Whatever the age, this ceremony and gathering of women will serve to celebrate the deceased woman's life. Modifications can be made accordingly if, instead of a group of women, there is one woman, or a family that wishes to celebrate the loss of a female.

Preparation Meeting and Preparation Period

Due to the nature of this ceremony, in the preliminary meeting, the ceremony process is reviewed and additions or adjustments made. The ceremony is clearly reviewed and each aspect tailored as needed to fit the circumstances and the participants' needs.

At this preparation meeting, the request is made for healthy eating, drinking, and physical self-care for the two days prior to the actual ceremony.

Assignment: The organizing participant is asked to have individuals joining in the ceremony journal their memories of the deceased and end by writing a letter to her, celebrating her life. Additionally, if elderly, they are asked to write about the Crone's wisdom. They are asked to bring flowers that are specifically chosen for the occasion; special in meaning to either the participant or the Crone. The organizing participant is asked to bring enough flowers to fill a small boat that will be draped in white cloth. She is asked if she would like to take the cloth home prior to the ceremony and decorate it to make it more personalized.

A note for the guide: This ceremony uses a 'boat' and the boat can be made of any material. However, if this ceremony will be conducted repeatedly, it should be made of sturdy materials.

The Beginning of the Ceremony

Upon arrival, there is an overall discussion about the flow of the ceremony and the participants are made physically comfortable. They may want to have some time to just talk with each other about the loss of the Crone.

As stated above, you, as guide, will explain that for Shamans the elements of Earth, Air, Fire, and Water are associated with the compass directions. The pairing of element with direction varies by Shamanic tradition. For this ceremony the pairings of direction with element are North-Earth, East-Air, South-Fire, and West-Water, which is common to the Celtic Shaman tradition. Six colored candles are brought forward: brown or green, yellow, red, blue, white, and purple. A compass is placed in a central spot so that all may be aware of the compass directions. Either you or the participants set the candles in their correct locations, with the brown or green one being placed in the North location, the yellow one in the East, red in the South, blue in the West, and white and purple placed in the center. All sit.

You explain that there will be Shamanic InWorld journeys and the participants will be asked to relax, close their eyes, and visualize the words that you say. Express also, that not all people visualize, but rather some sense, some feel, and some just listen; making sure that the participants know that there is no right and wrong to their experiences.

White washcloths are handed out and the participants told that they will use them later. They are directed to put the washcloths on their laps.

When ready, the ceremony begins with the lighting of the essential oils or incense, and then the candles in the following Shamanic Journey.

Shamanic Journey to Open the Ceremony: As you are breathing in a relaxed manner, begin slowing down the pace of the day, of yourself, and your Being. We will begin by diffusing the essential oils that were chosen (or if incense is used, modify wording accordingly).

(Pause while this is task is completed.)

Now we are going to light the ceremonial candles, and as we do so, we are opening our world here, to the Inner Realms and beginning to bring that energy here to us. We will do that by opening the directional-North, East, South, West-and elemental energies-Earth, Air, Fire, and Water, symbolizing that opening with the lighting of the candles. Are we ready? (If all affirm, continue.)

Again breathe slowly; and find yourself in a Central Area InWorld. There is a compass there and around you see the directions of North, East, South, and West. In each direction you will be seeing or sensing scenery, as I describe it.

First, we face to the North, and move towards the element of Earth. All around us is Earth. Mountains, rocks, canyons. A valley, with lush grass. A cave up ahead. Smell the Earth smells. Grass, trees, mud. We open our ceremony space to this energy and let it flow into this realm, like opening a giant curtain. We gently fling it open and the energy pours in to our ceremonial space. We light the green/brown candle, symbolizing this opening. And breathe in the Earth energy. (Either you or a participant lights the candle, with the others observing.)

Breathe slowly again; step back InWorld. And now we face East. To the element of Air. We open the curtains and we step into the Air. A light wind blows. Birds fly. Leaves blow. A wind storm you see furiously blowing in the distance. The crispness of spring. Like clothes on a clothesline lightly blowing in the breeze. And we invite the Air energy into this plane; lighting the yellow candle to symbolize the flow of Air energy to our realm. (Light candle.)

And now we open to the South, to the element of Fire. As we open these curtains we feel Fire as Summer, full

Sun. Hot. But not desperately so. Fire in a fire pit. With Fire energy dancing on the licks of the flames. Bask in the power of the Fire energy. Creativity. Volcano in the distance, birthing itself. The invisible waviness above a fire, all around us here; without heat, just the energy. Open to it fully and we invite it into our plane, lighting the red candle to symbolize its presence. (Light candle.)

Breathe slowly. And now to the West, to the element of Water. The curtains open and we see a pool of water, the sun setting on the ocean in the distance. A river. Rain. Water is all around. We invite this element, and light the blue candle to symbolize its presence here. (Light candle.)

Return to the Inner Realms, breathing slowly. And now we turn back to the Central area where we began, leaving all of the curtains open to allow the flow of the energy to continue. We breathe it all in. Looking North at Earth, then East at Air, South at Fire, and West at Water. What is left is Spirit, and we open to that. The Divine. Our Spirits. As we relax our Beings, and allow that to open, our energy flows out, mingles with the elemental energy, and the Divine. Both the Male Divine, the God-head, the Sun, as well as the female Divine, <u>our</u> Divine. The Moon, the goddess energy. Female energy. We invite the presence of Spirit and Higher powers to the ceremony and light the purple and white candles to symbolize this invitation. (Light candles.)

We breathe in all we have opened to, allow the presence of all, even though we now open our eyes. We allow all of the energy to remain with us...we open our eyes, but remain open to All.

The Ceremony Proper

The women are seated comfortably around the flower-filled boat draped with the white cloth and have a heartfelt discussion of the Crone's life, the celebration of it, and her wisdom. As that conversation draws to a close, the women are given an opportunity to modify their celebration letters to be more in line with what they are feeling after the discussion. Adequate time is given for any extra processing that needs to be done.

The guide will work to keep this a very positive experience, with focus on the wisdom imparted by the Crone and the celebrations of her life. If the ceremony is not for a Crone, but rather for a younger woman, the discussion would be modified accordingly. The point of this phase is a coming together as women and holding On High the Crone's life, her Being, and her Soul.

When the conversation is over, and the modifications are complete, the women move outside and light a fire in some sort of container or fire ring. Each participant reads aloud her celebration letter and puts it in the fire. While it burns, the guide makes a summary statement about the aspect of the Crone that is celebrated, held On High, and given to the Universe. She invites others to do so as well. She supports cheering and positive exclamation.

When complete, the women return inside. The guide brings the ashes from the letters and fire, making sure there are no embers. The participants are each given a candle.

The Shamanic Ceremony Journey (For this journey, sit around the boat that is full of flowers and has been draped in white fabric. Each woman holds the flowers she brought. The ashes, in a fireproof pot, are put in the boat as well.): Begin breathing in a relaxed manner, letting go of any thoughts that may pop into your head. Just know that thoughts will come, it is our nature. When they do, you will become aware of them, acknowledge that they are there, and just let them bubble up and away. Do not get down on yourself for it is a normal experience. So breathe in a relaxed manner. Letting the thoughts go as they arise. Breathe in ... out ... in ... out. And find yourself walking along a brook. I am walking with you. ... We are walking alongside the slow moving brook.

It bubbles, and slowly flows amongst the stones. As we walk, you feel every cell, and every one of your body processes, slowing, beginning to reset to the pace of the flow of the brook. ... To a comfortable, peaceful pace.

Up ahead there is a very shallow area, about 2 inches deep, with a nice bed of sand. We step in and feel the water. Feel the sand. It is a comfortable temperature.

As we breathe in, the bottom of our feet open, and up through our feet flows Water energy. Water energy is very cleansing and soothing and it cleanses us as it flows upwards. ... We breathe out, and toxins, and dust of the day, which is just the energetic residues that are created from normal life, flow out. ... We breathe in again, and the Water energy spirals and swirls higher ... and breathe out, the toxins and dust of the day, flow out down the brook. ... One more time in and the Water energy flows up to the top of your head ... and out, residues flow down the brook.

As you breathe the Water energy in and out slowly; and as it spirals within your Being, cleansing as it goes, you pick up the white washcloth from this realm. Back InWorld, you reach it down and soak it in the water of the brook. You walk to the shore and sit beneath a tree that is on the shoreline, with roots going right into the water. You lean with your back against the majestic tree, allowing your legs and feet to join with the tree roots, energetically connecting to the water you were just in.

As you lean back into the tree, you touch your fore-head with the washcloth, both InWorld and in this

The Death of the Crone

realm, cleansing your 3rd Eye, so that you may discern all that you 'see' intuitively, discern with wisdom. ... You wash your eyes so that you may see clearly in the Outer Realms. ... You wash your ears, so that you may hear without your ego interfering. ... You wash your mouth, so that you might speak clearly, kindly, and with love. ... And, you wash your heart, so that you feel and give love unconditionally.

We are now cleansed and ready to walk further. ... We step out of the water and head West. West is the direction of the element of Water. And Water is female. In the Heavens above, in the West, is the Moon. Also female. So we head to the female; the Divine Female; the mystical Divine. ...

After some time, we arrive in the West. There is a beautiful sunset; with dusk arriving. It is fall-like in the air, with some crispness, although not uncomfortable. But all around you sense Water. Ocean waves, the sea. A river flowing into the sea. Rain on the horizon. Dampness. A healing pool next to you.

Water is all around. Open yourself to feel it. ... Breathe it in. ... The Water energy mingles with your Being, which is mostly water. Flowing through you also is Female energy. The Female Water energy. ... Positive, solid but flowing delicately, but sturdily. You feel the positive nature of the mystical Divine Female.

Above us opens the Heavens, and the most glorious Moon light starts to fill the area we are in. It feels incredibly peaceful ... silky ... smooth ... creamy ... female ... pure. Peaceful.

You see a set of steps gently spiraling up to the Moon; the Full Moon. ... And down the steps walk the four Moon Beings, each representing a phase of the Moon: Dark, First Quarter, Full, and Last Quarter Moons. ... They are carrying the Crone, who is lying in their arms, as light as light could be.

It seems to take no effort for the Moon Beings to carry her down the steps. We watch as they do so. Step by step.

She is illuminated and you realize that it is her Being, and not her physical body, that they are carrying. Her Being. Her Soul.

You can tell that they are proud to be a part of this ceremony. They have heard all that we have said about her, and are honored to be here with us. And yet respectful of the occasion.

Finally, they have finished walking down the steps and they are making their way to the sea. We follow them.

Up ahead, we see that there is a small boat. As we get closer we see that they have spent time decorating it with images of what we had been saying in our cel-

ebration. You look closer and see different scenes, different feelings, and different wisdoms. You see images of which we spoke. (Longer pause)

The boat is full of flowers. The Moon Beings arrive and place her on the bed of flowers. They cover her with a feather light cloth. They invite us to, one by one, come and say our goodbyes.

After you do so, you place your flowers into the boat in front of you and then light your candle from the White and Purple candles that represent Spirit. (Give them time to do this.)

The Moon beings have waited for us to finish, and when we are done, they give a signal and the Universe opens up. Angels come; female angels. ... They come and come and come.

Filling the sky. And then they start singing. ... First one sings a solitary tone, then another, and another. ... One by one they join in singing solitary tones, till the Universe is full of their music. We listen for a moment. For a while. Reflecting on her as a woman.

The tones flow all around us. All around her. Until finally the vibration, the energy of the tones sets the canoe free. ...

The music continues and becomes so full that it lifts the canoe. Floating up to the heavens; to the Universe.

The music is so pure; and fills the canoe so full and her so full, that it illuminates the most iridescent light color till it becomes pure energy, losing all shape and form.

She has become one with the Universe. Her gifts and wisdom are not lost but become a part of All that there has been, and All that there will be.

We hold her On High and hold the candles up to the Heavens, to the All, the Nothing. And we Celebrate her Life. Her Being. And her Soul. Amen. (Extinguish the candles.)

The participants are then given an opportunity to process their experiences. Additionally, they are provided with dye and other art materials in order to personalize their washcloth that was used in the spiritual cleansing ritual. This way they have an outward sign of the ceremony that they have just completed.

The End of the Ceremony

After they are done writing, reflecting, and decorating their washcloths, they process the entire day, and then do the closing, and extinguish the candles. A celebration may follow.

Shamanic Journey to Close the Ceremony: As we opened the InWorld curtains and lit the candles, so must we close the curtains and extinguish the oils/incense and candles. Breathe in a relaxed manner and we find our-

selves back in the Central Area, like the center of the compass. We breathe in all that we have done today. All the feelings, sensations, experiences. ... We look North at the element of Earth, release the energy and close the curtain. We extinguish the brown/green candle to symbolize this closing. (Extinguish candle.)

We look East, at the element of Air, and let go of that energy, closing the curtain, and extinguishing the yellow candle. (Extinguish candle.)

We look to the South, to the element of Fire, and release that energy, closing the curtain, and extinguishing the red candle. (Extinguish candle.)

And we look to the West, to the element of Water, releasing that energy, with which we have spent much time today. Fondly letting it go, closing the curtain and extinguishing the blue candle. (Extinguish candle.)

We are left with Spirit. The Divine. Male and Female. Proud of Female. Deeply connecting to that energy. We will allow that connection to continue as we extinguish both the white and purple candles. We allow the Divine to flow within us. We hold our Beings On High and remain deeply connected to the Heavens, the Universe. Breathe this in as we begin to return to this day. This realm. This plane. And we open our eyes to the ordinary. Knowing where we have been and what we have done and what we can do. (Extinguish candles.)

Chapter 4

Thoughts and Musings

This guidebook illustrates that ceremonies can be written based on a general template derived from literature. This template includes a preliminary meeting that occurs at least two weeks prior to the ceremony, and in addition to gathering background information, assigns homework to be completed prior to the scheduling of the ceremony. All together, the preliminary meeting and homework set the intention for the ceremony as well as begin to mark it as an important, sacred event.

The ceremony day template includes a beginning of the ceremony, the ceremony proper, and an end to the ceremony.

This set of ceremonies is laid on a foundation of Shamanism. This foundation does not modify the template, but rather enriches it, making the ceremonies more powerful and deep. The Shamanic foundation is partly added by utilizing the Shamanic Journey format. Additionally, this foundation enables the participants to connect to other world energies by opening the flow of the elemental energies to our Earthly realm. This opening of the flow occurs in the opening of the ceremony, and then the energy is utilized within the ceremony itself. The energy flow is closed during the end of the ceremony.

By creating a Shamanic Ceremony template, the number of ceremonies one can construct is without limit, save for the adeptness of the Shaman or guide. Additionally, ceremonies can be modified for any unique circumstances that might arise. Journeys may also be modified depending on the Shaman's adeptness of creating permutations of actual journeys as presented above. If the Shaman has the road map, then there are no limits to either.

Given the template itself, Shamanic Ceremonies can be constructed beyond Rites of Passage ceremonies. In fact, a ceremony can be created instantaneously, except for the preliminary meeting. Given that the goal of that meeting is to create intention and begin to mark the importance and sacredness of the ceremony, those aspects would only need to be marked in a different manner.

A ceremony template is just that; a structure to guide the leader. As such, it will need to be modified to meet the requirements of the participants. But given that there is a template, it gives the guide the comfort to modify as needed.

Thus, Shamanic Ceremonies can be easily created for any occasion. They can be deeply moving and powerful. They can take ceremony to a new level, letting go of old ways of being and connecting to a new way of being, in a deep way. And they can begin to address what is lacking in our culture: female Rites of Passage ceremonies.

More Thoughts...

Yes, there is power in ceremony. And yes, there is even greater power when Shamanism is added and used as a foundation to that ceremony. That was, and is, one of the jobs of the Shaman; helping facilitate healing and growth in peoples' lives. But in our society, there is a greater need than just for ceremony.

Initially the thought was that an individual, family, or group would request a specific Rite of Passage ceremony, due to some internal need. The Shaman or guide would have an active practice of conducting ceremonies and even advertise as such. That Shaman or facilitator would utilize these templates and ceremonies depending on the life transition at hand.

But then, as I read, digested, and planned, I came to the sense that there is a bigger need in our society; bigger than the need for ceremony overall, or for ceremony for women's transitions. What came to me was the lack of a societal-supported gathering of women with the goal or the specific intention of supporting each other, both regularly, as well as through life transitions. What is missing is a societal-sanctioned method of women supporting women.

Based on my musings during the researching and readying for, and then the writing of this guidebook, I began formulating the composition of a women's group; a group intended to support each other, laugh with each other, cry with each other, and facilitate transitions with each other.

In the ideal world, the group that I would set up, if there were no limitations, would be as follows.

There is a group of women who meet monthly on the Dark Moon, or as close to it as possible. They are a cohesive group, putting aside separate identities as they step into the group community. They have a regular meeting place that is also open for use when an individual needs additional quiet or retreat time, such as during her monthly cycle.

There is a cyclically, rotating schedule of set-aside times for the above noted ceremonies so that twice a year there is a ceremony day for the coming to fertility, twice a year for coming of age, twice a year for the midlife transition, and twice a year for the transition to Crone. The ceremonies for the birth of a girl child or the death of a Crone are scheduled for an additional time or included at the next meeting. The other four meetings within the year would be for the equinoxes and solstices. Thus, monthly there would be a gathering of the women and a ceremony. These ceremonies would be one of the above six, or a variation of one of the six,

Thoughts and Musings

or one to celebrate the seasons. The ceremonies could be for group members, friends, or female family members.

The group though would go beyond the ceremony. That would be one aspect of the day.

A woman could be initiated into the group at any time upon adulthood. The monthly ceremony retreat day would focus on belonging and connectedness. So as to not feel rushed, it would be an all-day commitment. It would be a time to laugh, to cry, and to bond. The women would provide skills according to their strengths such as food, readings, and ceremony details. They would be equal in the process, no matter what the individual woman's role is. Together, and only together, they would make the day, the days, happen.

We are all guilty of rushing through life, not paying attention to the changes and transitions that we are going through. Many of us hold very little sacred. Suddenly, we have made it through the transitions in our life, often with emotional angst. Sometimes the angst is so great that it is obvious to others that something is wrong. With a group of women who are deeply connected we need not transition on our own. The Crones can mentor the younger women and the younger women can help the Crones feel more purpose in their lives. The younger women can impart youthful wisdom and yet gain deep wisdom from the Wise Women; women connecting, supporting, and honoring other women. Walking the walk with them and holding them on High, from Beginning to End.

Bibliography

IAmShaman.com. (2011). Retrieved January 2011, from IAmShaman.com: http://iamshaman.com/eshop/10Browse.asp?Category=Essential%20Oils

Altman, N. (2002). *Sacred Water: The Spiritual Source of Life*. Mahwah, New Jersey: Hidden Spring.

Arvigo, R., & Epstein, N. (2003). *Spiritual Bathing: Healing Rituals and Traditions from Around the World*. Berkeley, California: Celestial Arts.

Biziou, B. (1999). *The Joy of Ritual: Spiritual Recipes to Celebrate Milestones, Ease Transitions, and Make Every Day Sacred*. New York, New York: Cosimo.

Bonewits, I. (2007). *Neo Pagan Rites: A Guide to Creating Public Rituals That Work*. Woodbury, Minnesota: Llewellyn Publications.

Boylan, K. M. (2000). *The Seven Sacred Rites of Menopause: The Spiritual Journey to the Wise-Woman Years*. Santa Monica, California: Santa Monica Press.

Close, H. (2006). *Ceremonies for Spiritual Healing and Growth*. New York, New York: The Haworth Pastoral Press.

Eckert, R. P. (1998). Guidelines For Creating Effective Rites Of Passage. In L. C. Mahdi, N. G. Christopher, & M. Meade (Eds.), *Crossroads: The Quest For Contemporary Rites Of Passage* (pp. 251-269). Chicago, Illinois: Open Court.

Farmer, S. D. (2002). *Sacred Ceremony: How to Create Ceremonies for Healing, Transitions, and Celebrations.* Carlsbad, California: Hay House, Inc.

Grof, C. (1998). Rites of Passage: A Necessary Step Toward Wholeness. In L. C. Mahdi, N. G. Christopher, & M. Meade (Eds.), *Crossroads: The Quest for Contemporary Rites of Passage* (pp. 3-15). Chicago, Illinois: Open Court.

Horn, G. (2000). *The Book of Ceremonies: A Native Way of Honoring and Living the Sacred.* Novato, California: New World Library.

Hughes, K. W., & Wolf, L. (1997). *Daughters of the Moon, Sisters of the Sun: Young Women & Mentors on the Transition to Womanhood.* Stony Creek, Connecticut: New Society Publishers.

Ingerman, S. (2004). *Shamanic Journeying: A Beginner's Guide.* Boulder, Colorado: Sounds True, Inc.

Johnson, J. T. (2001). *The Thundering Years: Rituals and Sacred Wisdom for Teens.* Rochester, Vermont: Bindu Books.

Kern, H. (2000). *Through The Labyrinth: Designs and Meanings Over 5,000 Years.* New York, New York: Prestel.

Keville, K., & Green, M. (2009). *Aromatherapy: A Complete Guide to the Healing Art* (2nd Edition). Berkeley, California: Crossing Press.

L'am, D. (2006). *Becoming Peers: Mentoring Girls into Womanhood.* Sebastopol, California: Red Moon Publishing.

Lorler, M. (1998). *Shamanic Healing Within The Medicine Wheel.* Albuquerque, New Mexico: Brotherhood of Life, Inc.

Bibliography

Mahdi, L. C., Christopher, N. G., & Meade, M. (Eds.). (1996). *Crossroads: the Quest for Contemporary Rites of Passage.* Chicago, Illinois: Open Court.

Matthews, C., & Matthews, J. (2003). *Walkers Between The Worlds: The Western Mysteries From Shaman To Magus.* Rochester, Vermont: Inner Traditions International.

McBride, K. (2004). *105 Ways to Celebrate Menstruation.* Vacaville, California: Living Awareness Publications.

McColman, C. (2003). *The Complete Idiot's Guide To Celtic Wisdom.* New York, New York: Alpha Books.

McGarvie, I. (2009). *The Sweat Lodge is for Everyone: The Non-Native's Guide to Building, Participating in, and Benefiting from Native American Sweat Lodge Ceremonies.* Toronto, Ontario: Ancient Wisdom Publishing.

McKenna, T., & McKenna, D. (1993). *The Invisible Landscape: Mind, Hallucinogens, And The iChing.* New York, New York: Harper One.

Mumm, M. S. (2004). *The Rituals Resource Book: Alternative Weddings, Funerals, Holidays and Other Rites of Passage.* Ann Arbor, Michigan: Personal Growth Publishers.

Ratsch, C. (2005). *The Encyclopedia of Psychoactive Plants: Ethnopharmacology and Its Applications.* Rochester, Vermont: Park Street Press.

Walsh, R. (2010). *The World of Shamanism: New Views of an Ancient Tradition.* Woodbury, Minnesota: Llewellyn Publications.

Worwood, S., & Worwood, V. A. (2003). *Essential Aromatherapy: A Pocket Guide to Essential Oils & Aromatherapy.* Novato, California: New World Libraray.

Worwood, V. A. (1991). *The Complete Book of Essential Oils & Aromatherapy.* Novato, California: New World Library.

About the Author

Nancy Baker has Doctorates in both Psychology and Metaphysical Science. She is a licensed Psychologist, Clinical Hypnotherapist, Spiritual Director, Ordained Minister, Reiki Master, Spiritual Alchemist, Celtic Shaman, and organic farmer. Utilizing her skills she works deeply in the 'Other Realms' to facilitate healing and growth. She moves fluidly and knowledgably through the Inner Realms and works with the energies found there for teaching and healing; connecting deeply to the Other World energies of the Alchemists and Shamans.

Nancy resides in Central Pennsylvania, on her 14 acre farm. It is there where she, along with her training, learned to touch the Earth, and truly 'see,' never able to go back to the old ways. She opens her farm for retreats, from afternoons to weekends. The farm is a deeply spiritual place. Some say there is a portal there, out in the Spirit Ring, where the Labyrinth, Medicine Wheel, Kabbalah Tree of Life, and Pyramid are. Others have seen a female being out there; a loving kind being. All comment, upon arrival, at the deep sense of peace.

She now has a webpage, *EssenceOfSoul.com*, where she shares what she learns InWorld, inviting others to do the same.

From Nancy: Every Shaman has a tale to tell, about what led him or her, into Shamanism, and my life story is no different. Mine began in September 1999, 2 months after my hysterectomy. One day, out of the blue, I had, what the doctors' call, a pelvic deep vein thrombosis, which let loose and hit the front of my brain in a shower of emboli. What that means is that I had a stroke, but instead of one big clot, the clot broke up into little pieces, hitting the front of my brain in many places, causing multiple small lesions. It sounds horrible, and indeed, there were changes in me the moment it happened. However, with the stroke, the InWorld doors opened and suddenly I had this huge flow of energy released. With much guidance and training and mentoring, I learned how to open the doors to the InWorld and how to close them with intention, how to navigate the Inner Realms, and how to use the energies for healing.

Now the call deepens. It is time to step out. Teach. Learn. Put the pieces together. The world is in a time of transition. We can all play a role in healing ourselves, others, and the Earth. Learn as much as you can, from everywhere you can, so you too can be part of the solution.

This book is a result of that call. I hope both experienced and inexperienced individuals find it helpful. From the calling also came my webpage, *EssenceOfSoul.com*. Come and read, explore, learn, share, and connect.

About the Photographer

Susan Youshaw, of SLYphotography, has been interested in photography since she was a young teenager. She specializes in the creative aspects of photography; via picture, she brings out each subject's inner personality and unique story. She is able to take a client's basic description of the concept he or she is interested in, turning into a work of art.

She highly enjoys focusing on, finding and then creating photographic art that centers around spiritual issues. Hence, she was the perfect choice to create the cover for this book. The cover represents the main components of the ceremonies: the Water energy, the Moon energy, and the Goddess. She was able to put these elements together into a photographic work of art.

Besides designing book covers she also has designed photographic art for webpages. For examples of her work, please go to Nancy's webpage, EssenceOfSoul. com.

Susan has a Certificate of Professional Photography from New York Institute of Photography and has taken multiple photography courses, while working on her Photography degree from The Art Institute of Pittsburgh. To contact Susan, please go to EssenceOfSoul.com, About Us.

Printed in Poland
by Amazon Fulfillment
Poland Sp. z o.o., Wrocław